WHEN A CHURCH BECOMES A CULT

When a Church Becomes a Cult

The Marks of a New Religious Movement

Stephen Wookey

Hodder & Stoughton
LONDON SYDNEY AUCKLAND

First published in Great Britain 1996

10 9 8 7 6 5 4 3 2 1

British Library Cataloguing in Publication Data
A record for this book is available from the British Library

ISBN 0 340 65622 0

Printed and bound in Great Britain by
Cox & Wyman Ltd, Reading, Berks

Hodder and Stoughton Ltd
A Division of Hodder Headline PLC
338 Euston Road
London NW1 3BH

CONTENTS

INTRODUCTION

The cults are the unpaid bills of the church.[1]

A few years ago, shortly after I moved to London, I became aware of a new group on the London religious scene. It called itself a church. It was young, dynamic and outwardly successful. When the orthodox churches were weak and ineffectual, it by contrast was growing apace. It claimed to be orthodox in doctrine but somehow succeeded where the rest were falling. It was hard to criticise because it seemed to be doing the same job we were attempting – but with considerably more success.

But there was another side that became increasingly apparent. Although it claimed to be an orthodox Christian church, it also believed that everyone else was wrong. Nobody else was as keen as they were, or as committed. In fact nobody outside of their church was a Christian. Alarm bells started to ring.

Then stories started to come out: of members who had undergone personality changes, who had become so tied to the group that they were unable to make any form of decision without first asking their 'discipler'; of members who had found leaving the group an immensely difficult experience, both practically and emotionally.

And then there were the people who turned up at our church who had escaped. Often they would be gifted, able people. But the experience had undoubtedly scarred them. People in our own church were being approached in the streets and the Underground, and invited to Bible studies at this church. Others were being phoned every day, again being invited to meetings.

Still others went to the meetings and found them compelling, but were often left a little uneasy at the end.

Gradually I began to hear of similar stories from other churches and ministers. They too, it seemed, were increasingly disturbed by some of the situations they were encountering. The group was being banned from colleges and campuses, often causing problems for the existing religious societies and groups.

I started keeping a collection of articles, letters, and booklets relating to the group, which had by this time moved to several other cities both in the UK and beyond. Finally a friend asked me to write a little booklet expressing my reservations about this group, and where I believed they were going wrong.

Partly as a result of this, further opportunities arose to speak on the subject of cults and deviant religious groups, and the more I thought about it, the more I read, the more I became convinced that the problem was one that posed big questions both for the church and society. There were an enormous number of these groups springing up, more and more people were being caught up in them, and there was little, it seemed, anyone could do.

The Western world, over the last few decades, has witnessed an enormous increase in these groups. They are often full of young people, dynamic, committed, and with a strong moral code. In many ways they put to shame the prevailing ethos of cynicism and apathy. There is a clear sense of purpose and direction that is both admirable and refreshing. And yet there are always the questions: questions about finance and fundraising; questions about over-restrictive leadership; questions about mind-control or manipulation; questions even about sexual malpractice.

The rise in religious cults seems to have coincided with a corresponding fall in the influence of traditional Christianity. Every year statistics declare that numbers attending church on Sundays are declining. People are increasingly of the opinion that religious belief is on the way out. But at the same time there is this proliferation of religious cults.

It is true that to a large extent our society has thrown off a belief in traditional Christianity. The secular humanists of the earlier part of our century assured us that a belief in God was no longer either necessary or rational. Traditional religion was seen as outdated and dispensable. We were led to believe that it would usher in a new age of humanistic utopianism, free from the religious superstition and irrationalism.

But it was a false hope. Many of those who trumpeted the claims of humanism the loudest died deeply disillusioned. George Bernard Shaw wrote near the end of his life,

> The science to which I pinned my faith is bankrupt. I believed it once. In its name I helped destroy the faith of millions of worshippers in the temple of a thousand creeds. And now they look at me and witness the tragedy of an atheist who has lost his faith.[2]

But not only have the dreams of humanism proved illusory, religion itself has not released its group. Far from being set free, we are instead finding ourselves enslaved to new masters and new teachings. We are bombarded by religions, cults, philosophies, and therapies all clamouring for our attention and our support. Each claims to have something unique to offer, a special truth, a new understanding, a deeper knowledge, an inner peace which will prove the answer to our deepest longings. 'Are you a young person looking for a meaning in life? Are you a city businessman unable to withstand the pressures and stresses of work? Are you looking for someone or something to show you the way? If so, then we have the answer.'

In Charles Ferguson's *The New Books of Revelation* this point is made:

> It should be obvious to any man who is not one himself, that the land is overrun with messiahs. I refer not to those political quacks, who promise in one election to rid the land of evil, but rather, to those inspired fakirs who promise to reduce the diaphragm, or orient the soul through the machinery of a cult religion. Each of these has made himself the centre of a new

theophany, has surrounded himself with a brand of zealous apostles, has hired a hall for a shrine and then set about busily to rescue truth from the scaffold, and put it on the throne.[3]

It seems that the enormous dissatisfaction with the answers given by government, society or the Church is matched only by the desire for something else to fit into the vacuum. Those traditional bastions of authority can no longer be trusted, but we need something or someone else.

Here in central London, as I write, we are surrounded by devotees of Scientology, Hare Krishna, Mormonism, the Central London Church of Christ, and many others. They are sincere, devoted people. They claim to have found a purpose for their lives, they offer so much of what we think we are looking for – peace, success, contentment, wealth, happiness, direction. They offer an identity. They have much to attract us. They are surely to be applauded and welcomed.

And yet at the same time we know only too well that many of these sellers of religious wares are charlatans. Some have landed in prison on charges of embezzlement, others have been accused of the most appalling sexual abuse, still others have persuaded their members to join them in horrific mass suicide. Who can forget the almost unbelievable scenes of carnage from Jonestown, Waco or the Solar Temple in Switzerland? Indeed Waco and Jonestown have become a part of our language in much the same way as Aberfan or Piper Alpha, Bhopal or Hiroshima. They stand as savage reminders that all that glitters is not gold, that not all religious 'truth' is quite what it appears.

How, we ask, can so many intelligent, well-educated, and articulate people fall under their various spells? What makes them so powerful and attractive? Why cannot people see the obviously bogus claims of the religious gurus? Why, when they have thrown off Christianity on the grounds that it has an insufficient rational basis, are they prepared to embrace a philosophy or theology that all too often appears to have none?

But at the same time perhaps our society has never before laid

itself so open to these cults. We have embraced
that tells us that everything is relative, that there
truth, no real measure by which we can judge s
beliefs or world-view, no agreed standard. Everyone is entitled
to their own views. No one person's views should have more
authority than anyone else's. In the West we pride ourselves on
our free thinking.

The only view it is hard to hold today is the dogmatic one.
You can believe anything you like provided you do not suggest
anyone else is wrong or try to impose your views upon them.
Indeed tolerance is the order of the day. The only view we
cannot tolerate is the one that believes that some things are true
and others are false. But such a society lays itself wide open to
new and destructive philosophies, precisely because it refuses to
differentiate between them.

A man who will not stand for something is quite likely to fall
for almost anything.[4]

Truth is therefore no longer the issue. It is no longer the test to
which we subject a new teaching or philosophy. Indeed it is
almost regarded as a complete irrelevance. Now the issue is not
'Is it true?' but 'Does it work?'

In such a climate what right have we to criticise or undermine
the cults? If all religions are true if they are true for someone,
how can we criticise anyone else? What measure do we use? It
is no good today using the measure of truth, because truth,
objectively speaking, no longer seems to exist. So how can we
judge?

And yet everything in us cries out that we must. We see the
results of some of the cults, and although we have no philosophical framework with which to judge them, we know them to be
false and dangerous. We know we must be tolerant of those
who hold differing views to our own – indeed we must regard
their views as being as valid as ours – but at the same time we
do not really believe it. We want to know that what our hearts
tell us about the cults has some sound basis.

It comes down to our understanding of truth, and we must not lose confidence in truth. Indeed when people so confidently assert that they do not believe in absolute truth do they really believe it themselves?

The American writer Ravi Zacharias tells of how he was being shown around the Wexner Centre for the Performing Arts at Ohio State University. *Newsweek* magazine has branded the building the 'US's first deconstructionist building'.

> When you enter it you encounter stairways that go nowhere, pillars that hang from the ceiling without purpose, angled surfaces designed to create a sense of vertigo. The architect designed this building to reflect life itself – senseless and incoherent – and the capriciousness of the rules that organise the built world.

Ravi Zacharias had just one question to ask of the architect: 'Did he do the same with the foundation?'[5]

Of course not. If he had it would not have remained standing. And everyone knew it. It is then surely fair to ask questions about some of these religious cults. And questions not simply about their techniques, or their authoritarianism – dubious and deceitful though they may be – but about their foundations. Can their leaders claim to have received a message from God in any meaningful sense? What is their basis? Where does their authority come from? Are they internally consistent?

I write as a Christian who holds to a belief in absolutes. I accept the Jesus Christ revealed in the Bible, and believe it is He and He alone who can make sense of our world. I also believe that all too often it is because the Church has presented a false or watered-down view of this Christ that the world has so often chased after other gods. If the Church had been clearer in its proclamation and of more obvious integrity perhaps many of the cults would never have arisen, or at least attracted the number of devotees that they have. The existence of so many of the cults is in itself a testimony to the failure of the Church. They have stepped in where the Church has failed.

But there is another question that the Church must confront. Many of those groups now regarded universally as cults started out as mainline churches. David Berg of the Children of God, now the Family, attended the Bible Training Institute in Glasgow. His early followers were welcomed in churches as genuine Christians. Jim Jones was a recognised Nazarene pastor in the Southern USA before setting up Jonestown in Guyana. David Koresh did much of his proselytising among the Seventh Day Adventist churches of the UK. I happened to be speaking at the Seventh Day Adventist college in Bracknell the day Waco went up, and some of those who died, including Koresh himself, were known to students and staff.

Since then of course we have faced the tragedy of the Nine O'Clock Service in Sheffield, England. This book in fact was half-written when the news broke about the abuse and authoritarianism of that group. It thus presented something of a dilemma. I could not ignore the issue, particularly when so many of the characteristics of the church were precisely those that concerned me the most. At the same time I had no desire to score easy points at the expense of a group of people who were attracting quite enough attention already. I can only say that this book was not written in the aftermath of the NOS situation, nor was it meant to make cheap publicity out of it. I knew a little of the NOS before its demise became public, but only a little, and I am not qualified to speak about it in any depth. But if there are lessons to be learned from the NOS, we would do well to heed them. For it forces us to ask fundamental questions about all such groups.

How can these things happen? At what stage did these people cross the line? When did their churches become cults? Are there lessons for the churches to learn that will prevent others following in their footsteps? There are in fact a number of churches today that come close to exhibiting many of the traits of these groups, and we must not be complacent. 'There is nothing new under the sun'.

But the cults present a challenge for the world as well as for the Church. Contemporary thinking has it that one philosophy is as good as any other. And yet we see all too clearly the awful dangers of some of the cults. You do not have to be a Christian to believe that Waco and Jonestown were disasters waiting to happen. Many are the parents, brothers and sisters, husbands and wives who have seen their loved ones systematically stripped of their independence, their dignity and their life savings, and watched helplessly from the sidelines. Can we at once believe that all religions are of equal validity and then watch our own loved one being destroyed by one?

The aim of this book is to give something of a rule whereby we can judge the so-called cults. It is not my aim to write off all other religious systems simply because I am a Christian myself, although I do believe absolutely in the uniqueness of Jesus Christ. Rather I would like to present something of a framework which will enable Christian and non-Christian alike to make a clear judgment about a particular group.

As I have thought over the whole subject I have become aware that there is no really clear distinction between a church and a cult. There is only a continuum, a line that at some stage gets crossed. It is to the abiding shame of many who call themselves Christians that the line has so often been crossed.

But let us also be aware that it is a growing problem. There is in many people the subconscious feeling that it could never happen to them or to any of their friends. And yet, as we will see, it is often those we would never suspect of falling for the deceits of some of these movements who do get caught up. It is far more common than we realise.

Every day seems to bring news of another group, or cult, of lives ruined and families divided. Court cases abound and controversy reigns. And in a world where everything is OK we should not expect otherwise. It is the price we pay for religious and philosophical pluralism.

It is my contention therefore that we cannot treat the cults as simply an issue about abuse of authority. Unquestionably that is the defining mark of cults, but I do not believe that it is the fundamental cause. In the aftermath of the NOS many people have claimed that it is simply an issue of abuse. Great idea, shame about the abuse. But I do not believe that is sufficient. The Bible makes very great play on the fact that what we believe affects the way we think. In the cults we see that this is the case. The exercise of authority stems from a belief in where authority resides – which is a theological issue rather than a pastoral one. It is because a Jim Jones or a David Koresh has managed to persuade his followers that he is a unique conduit for God's revelation that he is able to exert such control over them.

This has two implications. First we will find it very hard to combat the cults unless we are prepared to take them on theologically. So often people shy away from this in the belief that it is not doctrine that matters but practice. If we cannot refute the doctrine, however, we have little basis for attacking the practice. By what standard can we attack the cults? What criteria can we use? Hence we have to come back to the Bible's insistence that belief to some degree determines behaviour. It is an idea that is anathema to the modern mind, but I do not believe we can avoid it. Dr Lee Belford, a professor of comparative religions, has written:

> The problem is essentially theological where the cults are concerned. The answer of the Church must be theological and doctrinal. No sociological or cultural evaluation will do. Such works may be helpful, but they will not answer the JW or Mormon, who is seeking biblical authority for either the acceptance or rejection of his beliefs.[6]

But second, we have to have a firm set of beliefs ourselves. We have already said that our society has difficulty in criticising the beliefs of another. This will always remain the case until we establish what we believe ourselves. In my discussions with parents or friends of those involved in the cults it is much easier to talk when we have an agreed basis of belief from which to argue.

This is, I believe, vitally important because of two beliefs that underpin much of our society today, and have deeply affected thinking within the Church. I have already mentioned them both, and they will appear many times before the end of the book. The first is the absolute abhorrence of dogma and certainty. Indeed the very words have become pejorative in themselves. As we have already said, certainty is despised as being arrogant, and dogma is scorned for its very narrowness. Distinctions do need to be made, however. It it not dogma or certainty that we should abhor, but a narrow, unthinking stridency of opinion that neither listens to other opinions, nor even acknowledges them. It is the difference between absolutes and absolutism. Charles Colson makes this distinction in his book *Who Speaks for God?*

> There's a world of difference between absolutes and absolutism . . . every time you tack 'ism' onto a term you change its meaning. Think of the word 'individual' – a good word suggesting individual dignity and worth. But 'individualism' denotes something altogether different – an egotistic mentality that puts individual interests above everything else . . . There's a huge difference between material and materialism, human and humanism, feminine and feminism. So Christians ought to boldly maintain the reality of absolutes. But that doesn't mean we are absolutist in our mentality. A belief in absolutes simply means we believe there is a created order. That there are virtues – like courage, fortitude, and patience – which are morally obligatory . . . Believing those things doesn't make you an absolutist . . .[7]

We must not be ashamed of a belief in absolutes, in believing certain things are true and others are false. In fact almost everyone does believe in absolutes. They may not be the same absolutes, but they still exist. When a relativist declares that all things are relative, that in itself is an absolute statement. Otherwise it loses any meaning it might have.

The other idea, very popular today, is that truth is less important than success. This sort of religious pragmatism has affected much of the Church. All kinds of religious programmes are advertised on the basis of their success, rather than their faithfulness to a particular understanding of truth. What immediately follows is a form of religious faith that is dominated by what the market will buy. Everything is packaged in such a way as to make it as attractive as possible with much more concern given to presentation and success than the product itself. David Wells has expressed this dilemma very clearly in *God in the Wasteland*.

Success is not an adequate criterion for either truth or wisdom. In fact, what is now occurring ... is a set of substitutions that might well have a lethal effect on the practice of historic Christian faith. Technique is being substituted for truth, marketing action for thought, the satisfaction of the individual for the health of the church, a therapeutic vision of the world for a doctrinal vision ... organism [is being substituted] by organisation, those who can preach the Word of God by those who can manage an organisation, the spiritual by the material.[8]

That is the thinking of the cults, as we shall see, whose only aim is to get people into their group. But it is the situation in which the Church now finds itself. Having to compete against the rival attractions of television, video, computer games and the Internet – and of course the religious cults – instead of concentrating on the truth that truly 'sets free' (John 8:32) we have instead given ourselves to compromising both product and presentation to the spirit of the age. I accept that we must always see how we can present truth in as relevant and interesting a way as we can, but it must never be at the expense of clarity. Faithfulness to truth is far more important than any relevance, perceived or real, to contemporary society.

1

THE DEFINITION OF ERROR

*'When men cease to believe in God, they don't believe
in nothing, they believe in anything.'*
G. K. Chesterton

The *Daily Telegraph* of 16 March 1995 carried this report:

> At a Cults and Counselling Conference last year, it was
> revealed that Britain is home to more than 500 religious cults,
> with around 500,000 believers but this looks like a conserva-
> tive estimate. There are almost 2,000 groups on the database
> of INFORM (Information Network Focus on Religious
> Movements) – from the London Church of Christ to flying
> saucer 'worshippers.'

There are, it seems, any number of different religious groups or
cults around. But what *is* a cult? It is a word often bandied
about, but what does it actually mean?

There are certain words in current usage which, although not
originally pejorative in themselves, have become so over time.
One thinks in a religious context of the word 'Puritan'. Historically it was the collective term for a group of devout Christian
leaders of the sixteenth and seventeenth centuries. Over the
years, however, it has come to take on a quite different aspect.
It is now used to denote the very worst sort of moralistic,
judgmental and narrow-minded hypocrite. One might say the
same of the word 'fundamentalist'. When it was coined early
this century it was meant to denote a person who believed in

the fundamentals of Christianity, as against the liberal thinking of the age. Today it is used to describe an unthinking and irrational religious bigot.

In many ways the word 'cult' has suffered a similar fate. Originally the word simply referred to a religious practice or 'cultus'. It could be in a temple or church, it might refer to a service or ceremony – but there was nothing in the word itself that was derogatory. Indeed the *Oxford English Dictionary* describes a cult as a 'System of religious devotion; devotion, homage to person or thing; fad, passing fancy, for some particular thing'. It was simply descriptive of a particular activity, a service or act of worship.

In time, however, it has come to be used to describe certain deviant religious groups such that to be labelled a cult is to invite ridicule and contempt. So perhaps it would be worth starting with a few definitions so that it will be at least clear how I will use the word.

For a start, cults can be of both a religious and non-religious variety. My own experience has been almost entirely with groups of a religious nature, but many of the same principles will apply to both. In any case when we boil things down we tend to find that even the religious cults are not so much religious movements as exercises in power and authority. Members may well be taken in by high-sounding spiritual talk, but very often the leaders are extremely cynical, using members simply for their own ends – financial, sexual, egotistic – to such an extent that it is hard to believe their religious claims are anything more than a front. But since my aim is to tackle religious cults that is where I will concentrate.

Broadly speaking, when we think of religion in general, we use a number of categories. We talk of the great religions of the world – Judaism, Hinduism, Islam, Buddhism, Christianity, etc. Then within the religions we talk of denominations, or sects. Usually a denomination will be mainstream and widely accepted, whereas sect denotes a relatively small, perhaps eccentric group, which has to some extent rebelled against or refused to conform to the larger group. But both words refer to a subsection or subgroup of the main religions. Hence the Anglican Church, of which I am a member, is a denomination within the Christian world.

Finally we talk of cults, usually meaning by the use of the word a group that is off mainstream theologically, but also deviant in practice. The most widely recognised trait of the cult is the use of some form of manipulation. But it is important to note that there is no clear definition, nor demarcation line. The words 'sect' and 'cult' are often used interchangeably. Indeed many commentators are unhappy with using the word cult at all. They prefer to substitute the more neutral phrase 'new religious movements' on the basis that we are not in a position to judge the 'cults'.

Even those with very clear and fixed views about the cults recognise the difficulty of words. The American writer Ronald Enroth, who has written widely on the subject, quotes Thomas Robbins in his book *A Guide to Cults and New Religions*:

> The term cult is applied to a disparate collection of groups and movements, and consequently has become unsuitable as a precise legal or social scientific category . . . In effect a 'cult' is any group stigmatised as a 'cult'.[1]

The word cult is thus a shade misleading and confusing. A cult is seen as a cult simply because someone chooses so to describe it, and while the word may be unsuitable it is the one with which we are stuck.

I am often asked about certain groups, whether I would describe them as cults. It is very often hard to say, because there is no clear dividing line, with cults on one side and mainstream religious groups on the other. Rather it is a continuum, with groups that start as orthodox moving until they reach a point where they can be accurately labelled as cults. Equally there are other groups that, while originally labelled as cults, have since moved into the mainstream (the Mormons might be an example). So while I am fairly clear in my own mind about groups that I do believe have crossed the line, I prefer to outline principles and leave people to decide for themselves. But for the purposes of this book let me attempt a few definitions. Broadly speaking we can talk about five main characteristics.

Authoritarianism

This is the first and most important feature of the cults. They all depend on heavy, charismatic – using the word in its non-theological sense – and authoritarian leadership. When we come to look at the roots of the individual cults we will see that they almost invariably start with an individual taking upon themselves powers and authority beyond the bounds of normal leadership. From that moment the group is defined by the personality and teaching of that particular person. That personality is stamped upon the group, to such an extent that the leader is able to demand a respect, and obedience from members that would not be tolerated in normal circumstances.

As Ronald Enroth has put it:

Abusive churches, past and present, are first and foremost characterised by strong, control-oriented leadership. These leaders use guilt, fear, and intimidation to manipulate members and keep them in line. Followers are led to think that there is no other church quite like theirs and that God has singled them out for special purposes. Subjective experience is emphasised and dissent is discouraged. Many areas of members' lives are subject to scrutiny. Rules and legalism abound. People who don't follow the rules or who threaten exposure are often dealt with harshly. Excommunication is common. For those who leave, the road back to normalcy is difficult.[2]

It is perhaps this authoritarianism that is most frightening. Again and again we will notice that wherever authority is supposed to reside – and religious cults will often refer to the Bible, or other outside sources – it is clear that ultimate authority always resides with the leader.

There are many ways in which this authority is exercised, and we will consider some of those later in greater detail. But there is often a very strict hierarchical structure whereby the leader is able to impose authority, whether through shepherding, discipling, or group pressure. There is often a leadership cult, such that members are completely in awe of those above them. There is often too a deliberate distance placed between the member and the leader. The leader is expected and allowed to live at a level of luxury or opulence barely dreamt of by members.

We are all familiar with Lord Acton's famous dictum, 'Power tends to corrupt. Absolute power corrupts absolutely.' When one reads the extravagant claims made about the leadership within the cults it is hard not to see the wisdom of the comment. If ever there is absolute power exercised today it is within some of the more extreme cults.

Elitism

Another striking feature of the cults is the belief that they and they alone are right. Everything is therefore seen in terms of a struggle between good and evil, everyone in the group being good, and everyone outside the group being evil.

This is of course a natural extension of the previous point. Given that the leader is so perfect, it can only mean that their teaching is also infallible. As a result there is a deep conviction within the cult member that this group is the sole purveyor of truth. The fact that there are thousands of such groups around the world believing precisely the same thing is neither here nor there.

Listen to the words of Brigham Young:

No man or woman in this dispensation will ever enter into the Celestial Kingdom of God without the consent of Joseph Smith . . . Every man must have the certificate of Joseph Smith Junior, as a passport to their entrance into the mansion where God and Christ are . . . He reigns there as supreme a being in his sphere, capacity and calling, as God does in His heaven.[3]

This élitism is both an attraction and a disadvantage for the group. Although we all want to be part of the select few, we are uneasy about writing off everybody else. Consequently the cults often make this very élitism, and detachment from the rest of society, an article of faith. Listen to the words of Frank Sandford of the Shiloh community:

> First you will be out of joint with the world, then out of joint with the professed Christian world, then out of joint with consecrated people, and then sanctified people, and then people that believe in Divine Healing, and then the Holy Ghost people you know, and then you will find a few other people who have gone on alone with God.[4]

In other words, only an élite few will ever make it to the summit, will ever truly 'go on alone with God'. All others will have fallen by the wayside. Consequently we expect others not to accept the teaching, and to reject us if we embrace the faith. There is already a built-in defence mechanism. Of course this also gives a ready-made excuse whenever anyone leaves the group. They just did not have the right commitment.

Again, there is something very atttractive about belonging to the only group or movement that fully knows the truth. It gives an identity, a significance to otherwise humdrum lives. We all want to be in on a secret. But by the same token this sort of thinking also explains why others refuse to accept their teaching and oppose them. These opponents do not have the truth, they are not part of the enlightened few. On the contrary, they belong to the enemy forces who are trying to bring them down. This in turn explains why there is such paranoia within so many of these groups.

Further we can readily understand why it can be so painfully difficult to leave such a group. Not only has it become the centre of one's life and personality, it is also the only truth. To leave the group is therefore to reject the truth with all its accompanying consequences.

When I left the group, I experienced hell. I felt an unbearable separation from God. I felt that God had left me, that I was divorced from someone I was deeply in love with. My whole life was over. I felt like a floating cloud. I felt extreme guilt over leaving my 'family' and betraying those I loved. I felt that God would kill me . . . I used to take long drives and just scream as loud as I could, the pain and the guilt were unbearable.'[5]

This is something that cult leaders are not slow to exploit. If a member is courageous enough to suggest that they feel like leaving the church, they are liable to face the most appalling pressure to stay.

The End Justifies the Means

The moment a member buys into the idea that this group alone is right, it is only a short step to believing that any method of recruitment is acceptable. This deceit, for deceit it is, can take many different forms.

It may simply mean that the pleasant and friendly person you might meet on the street collecting for world unity will be very loath to admit that they are member of the Unification Church. On one occasion it took me at least ten minutes before I could persuade one such collector to admit she was a Moonie. Such tactics are clearly part of their overall strategy, rather than the embarrassment, or over-eagerness of one individual member. One ex-Moonie explained it like this:

People would buy items from us because they thought they were donating to a charitable cause. Our consciences had been programmed by Moon'a value system. We told people we were sponsoring Christian youth programmes: a lie. We told them we operated drug rehabiliation houses: another lie. On the spur of the moment we told them anything that we thought would work. Since we thought we were saving the world from evil and establishing God's kingdom on earth was the most important effort on earth, we didn't look at it as 'real' lying.[6]

In fact the Moonies have been known to operate under at least 380 different names. Among them are these: the International Relief Friendship Foundation, the International Cultural Foundation, the International Conference on the Unity of the Sciences, the International Religious Foundation, the New Ecumenical Research Association, the Assembly of the World's Religions, the Universal Ballet Company, the New York City Symphony Orchestra, the *Washington Times*, and the *New York City Tribune*. Anyone could be forgiven for not realising they were all a front for the deceits of the Rev. Moon.

Many other deceits are used. Perhaps the most extreme form was that practised by members of the Children of God, now known as the Family. Their young women engaged in what came to be known as 'flirty fishing' – effectively offering sexual services to draw people in. In each case the overall thinking is simply pragmatism: if it works, we will do it.

In fact lying seems so fundamental a feature of some of these groups that we will consider it at greater length later. Again, it can take many forms. Indeed one of the most extraordinary features of cults is the way in which they appear able to hold beliefs that are directly contradictory to one another, or at the very least ignore unpalatable truths.

A classic example of this is Mary Baker Eddy, founder of the Christian Science movement. Within the thinking and teaching of the movement, suffering is really illusory and should not be accepted. This has of course caused innumerable problems for those in need of urgent treatment – some have died in refusing to accept that their illness or injury was real. What is particularly extraordinary about the movement is that while Mary Baker Eddy was propounding these ideas she was herself actually receiving frequent treatment for a long-standing malady.

In his book *Kingdom of the Cults*, Walter Martin comments:

The Christian Science Church has known for many years that though Mary Baker Eddy spoke vigorously against doctors and drugs as well as vigorously affirming the unreality of pain, suffering and disease, she herself was frequently attended in her declining years by doctors, received injections of morphine for the alleviation of pain, wore glasses and had her teeth removed when they became diseased. However the Christian Science Church insists upon the validity of Mrs Eddy's teachings which deny the very practices she herself exemplified.[7]

There are numerous other examples of groups or organisations that teach one thing but live another. But of course within their own frame of reference such a thing is unimportant.

Financial Dishonesty

Perhaps it is inevitable that any group that has a non-accountable leadership, and that believes the end justifies the means, will be susceptible to financial temptation. Given that materialism is the predominant spirit of the age, it is barely surprising that the new religious movements will reflect this.

Perhaps this needs a little underlining. All of us are to some extent children of our times, and are liable to reflect the values and thinking of society around us. Religion has traditionally stood against this trend, in particular by pointing to values and ideas that are claimed to be timeless. So we see Islam taking a strong public stand against much of the modern morality of the secular West, by pointing to the, as they see it, timeless values embodied in the Koran. Similarly the Christian Church has tried to offer an alternative to the secularist materialism all round us. And Christians have done so by pointing to the teaching of the Bible.

But within the new religious movements or cults a new authority has arisen, that of the leader or teaching of the group. Although many groups do claim to believe in the authority of the Bible, effectively the teaching of their particularly guru has superseded the Bible's authority. Since the leader does not sit under the Bible's authority or that, of say, the Koran, he can be answerable only to himself, because he is the possessor of this new authority. Consequently we frequently find the leadership justifying, teaching or practising a morality that is ultimately a reflection of the prevailing morality of society.

We could give many instances of this habit. All too often we notice that leaders of these movements live in a luxury that is not only far beyond the reach of their followers, but that is also offensive to the world around. An obvious example would be the Bhagwan Shree Rajneesh, who is rumoured to have possessed somewhere between twenty-six and ninety Rolls-Royces in which he was driven around his estate every day.

But examples need not be so glaring. One only has to note the number of new religious movements that have been under investigation for their financial affairs. The Rev. Moon was sent to prison for eighteen months in 1984 in the US for unpaid taxes. Again and again it seems that when members of religious groups accord infallible status upon their leaders, they are used to provide for the material benefit of those leaders, without any advantage to themselves.

Money is collected for fraudulent purposes – unity among churches, world mission, etc. – and the money usually only lines the pockets of the leadership. Members themselves are given only a pittance, their labour being for the most part unpaid.

Before moving on perhaps we should note that a number of Christian churches exhibit something of the same obsession with money. Indeed in some circles there has developed a whole theology that both applauds the accumulation of wealth, and provides a means of attaining it. So-called Christian teachers are totally unashamed in their appeals for money, and declarations that all people who follow God truly should be wealthy. Here is just a small selection of their comments.

The Christians should be the wealthiest people on earth . . . Do you have a financial mountain in your life? Start talking to your money. Tell your checkbook to line up with God's

Word. Talk to your business. Command customers to come into your business and spend their money there. Talk to the mountain ... I am sick and tired of hearing about streets of gold. I don't need gold in heaven, I got to have it now ... I don't know where these goofy traditions creep in, but one of the goofiest ones is that Jesus and His disciples were poor. Now there's no Bible to substantiate that ... the Bible says that He has left us an example that we should follow His steps. That's the reason I drive a Roll-Royce. I'm following Jesus' steps.[8]

One of these supposed Christian teachers has even written a book, entitled *How I Learned Jesus Was Not Poor*. Another so-called Bible teacher, on a recent tour of this country – a man respected in many circles for his seeming spiritual power – made a twenty-five minute appeal for money in one of his services. Suffice to say that the Bible does not teach that Jesus was rich, nor that His followers had any right to expect to be rich themselves.

It is extraordinary how many of these groups eventually come to grief in the area of finance. Obviously for the leaders the lure of riches is very powerful, and when they have a group of members willing to give anything for the cause the opportunity is there too. It is just another example of the corrupting influence of power.

Psychological Manipulation

This is undoubtedly the area that has most caught public attention, and with which the cults are most associated. It is also perhaps the area where we need to tread most carefully. Expressions such as brainwashing, mind-control, psychological manipulation, hypnosis, are freely bandied about without being clearly defined.

The idea or technique of brainwashing came to the fore during the Korean War, when American servicemen were cap-tured and subjected forcibly to programmes which sought to convince them that the Americans were wrong, and their enemies right. Since then the expression brainwashing, at least in a technical sense, has been used almost exclusively to refer to situations where some form of physical coercion has been applied. A more recent example would be that of Patty Hearst, daughter of the American newspaper tycoon, Randolph Hearst, whose support for the Symbionese Liberation Front – an obscure terrorist organisation – was gained through force. She was kidnapped by members of the group in 1974, locked in a dark closet for weeks, and systematically starved and raped. Later she seemingly became an active and convinced member of the group. She was even given a new identity, 'Tania', and was made to believe that the FBI would shoot her on sight.

When we come to cults or new religious movements, however, one rarely finds the use of physical force. The coercion used is of a different kind. Indeed even the use of the word coercion would be disputed by some who claim that no adult ever gets involved in a cult without their own willing participation. But there can be little doubt that certain techniques are used by these groups in order to persuade people to join a group they would not otherwise identify with.

One of the first and most obvious of these is group pressure. We are by nature communal animals, we exist in relationship. It is natural therefore that we want to make a good impression, to fit in, to please others. The cults use this to their own ends. Much work is done in groups, and often the individual is allowed little time on their own to think or analyse. Because the group seems so convinced of something the individual feels compelled to go along with it for fear of spoiling it for everyone else. Much of the work of recruitment is done on weekends away in an atmosphere of love, acceptance, and strong pressure. Ex-members frequently testify to the powerful influence of group members putting excessive pressure upon them in situations where it was difficult to withstand.

This brings us to a second technique, that of removing people from their ordinary spheres. Very often the first involvement with a cult will lead to a weekend away, or some form of retreat. Nothing wrong with that in itself, but for the fact that by taking people out of their normal orbit they are that much more susceptible to pressure. This is also done by persuading an individual to join one of their communal houses, where independent thinking and action becomes almost impossible. One ex-member of a group in London lived for a time in a two-bedroomed house with thirteen others!

Another similar feature of cults is that of 'love-bombing'. Few groups would go as far as the flirty fishing of the Family, but love-bombing is a common tactic used to draw people in. A member is made to feel that they are deeply and unconditionally loved – for many, a profound and unique experience – they are hugged often, told what a great person they are, and how much they have to offer. This appeals both to an individual's vanity and also to their insecurity. The love is very far from unconditional, however, as anyone attempting to leave the group will soon realise. All pressure can be brought to bear, and life made utterly miserable for the one who wishes to leave. Love is withdrawn and replaced by an almost demonic anger.

Another method of controlling an individual is the use of heavy discipling or shepherding. In this practice every disciple is given their own discipler. This person takes responsibility for the spiritual well-being of the disciple. Such responsibility often goes far beyond the spiritual sphere. In many groups the discipler will make decisions in almost every area of one's life – where one should live, what job one should do, whom one should marry. Indeed, as mentioned before, not to obey one's disciplier is equivalent to not obeying God.

But notice how this practice has at least two knock-on effects. It is a brilliantly effective means of exercising control, and passing on lessons. But it also has the effect of rendering the individual almost incapable of making decisions themselves. I have known extremely able people totally floundering when they have left a cult because suddenly they have had to get used to making independent choices again.

Another common technique used within the cults is that of food or sleep deprivation. As we will see later, this is cleverly done so that the individual is quite unaware that it is a deliberate ploy. When individuals are without proper sleep for any length of time, or when they do not have a sensible diet, they are much easier to influence.

Because cults are often about the understanding, use, and abuse of power it follows that all forms of control will be used upon members in order to gain and exercise that power. Some of these techniques are more obvious and dangerous than others. Most will certainly be used in groups other than those we refer to as cults. That is not to defend them, simply to state that any leader of any kind of group is capable of misusing the power entrusted to them. What sets the cults apart is that there seems to be a deliberate and systematic abuse of people over a period of time, in order to gain control, then, having gained it, to misuse it. Whether we call it mind-control, manipulation or even brainwashing is really incidental. What matters is that there is a definite attempt to manipulate people into making decisions that in their more lucid and rational moments they would not otherwise make.

I have mentioned five specific areas that might be seen as marking out a cult. Just recently I spent some time with a member of the Church of Scientology. He had become progressively disillusioned with the group and wanted to know how he could extricate himself. Of particular concern was the feeling of emptiness he would feel once he left. How could he hope to fill the vacuum? We talked in general about cults. He asked me what made a cult. I mentioned these five characteristics – authoritarian leadership, élitist mentality, doubtful use of money, use of deceit, and use of some form of mind-control. I asked him whether that rang any bells with the Church of Scientology, whether they fell into any of those categories. They were guilty of every one, he replied.

There are a number of other features that we will touch on later, but which are always associated with the cults. One is the way they often separate an individual from his or her family. Another is paranoia. Many cults see things in an apocalyptic way. The world will soon come to an end, they are engaged in a final, definitive war of good versus evil, and all who stand against are evil. Nobody outside of the group can be trusted. There is always some conspiracy theory about. It is always a help to have an enemy upon whom everything can be blamed, whether it be parents, society or national government. Indeed it has been said that all true cults need a text, an enemy, and an Armageddon. An individual I know, who has had connections with cult organisations in the past, eptomised this for me after the appalling explosion in Oklahoma City. I received a note from him, suggesting that it had all been the work of the FBI! But notice that there is no disproving a conspiracy theory. If there is no evidence for it, it shows how clever the conspiracy is. If certain things do seem a little strange, then that simply proves the truth of it.

Again if you look carefully at a cult you will often find there is no fringe. Because someone is either in or out, there is little room for doubters, half-hearts or fringe members. It has been wisely said that a church without a fringe is a cult.

One could point to their careful recruitment only of those they see as potential workers in the future – students, young up-and-coming business people – with no time for others seen as less successful or able. One group even criticised members for bringing in the wrong sort of recruits.

But there is one final mark that needs mentioning, even if it is one that those from a non-Christian background will perhaps disagree with. It is that the cults frequently take traditional, orthodox Christianity and pervert it. In other words this final characteristic refers not so much to a practice as to a belief.

It is customary today to separate practice from doctrine, belief from behaviour. There is a widespread feeling that it does not matter what you believe, provided that you do not browbeat others, or act dishonestly in the process. In other words what you believe is unimportant, but how you believe it is vital.

But we cannot make such a neat distinction. There is no such obvious demarcation. In the New Testament one of the funda-mental tenets is that what we believe inevitably affects the way we behave. Belief changes behaviour. If you study the letters of St Paul you will find that he always begins with doctrinal statements before he turns to aspects of behaviour. If the belief is right, argues Paul, then the practice will follow.

The centre of the Christian faith has always been the cross. When we understand the cross, then we understand the gospel, the Christian faith. The cross teaches both that there is nothing we can do to *earn* our salvation, and that there is nothing we can do to *add* to our salvation. It is for this reason that the New Testament speaks of the once-for-all nature of the death of Jesus (e.g., 1 Pet. 3:18; Heb. 7:27), and of the faith that his death inaugurates (Jude 3). Nothing else is necessary for our salvation – no new works, no new knowledge, no new teaching, no new experience. Yet it is precisely here that the cults fall down. Each of them adds something else to the revelation of God, so that there is something else we must do, or grasp, in order to be saved, whatever that might mean.

It follows from this that one of the clearest indications of a group going astray from the Christian faith is when the cross becomes less central or even incidental to its teaching. If the cross is no longer the heart of the message, something else will be, and it will be something other than the teaching of the Bible. The Rev. Moon teaches that the cross was a mistake, that God changed his mind in the Garden of Gethsemane. Herbert Armstrong teaches that the work was only begun on the cross: 'People have been taught, falsely, that "Christ completed the plan of salvation on the cross" – when actually it was only begun there'9; but unless the cross is central another gospel will invariably come in.

Of course, this is not to argue that any group that does not teach the Bible's message of the cross is a cult. But it is to say that where the cross is central there is less reason to fear, because the emphasis will always be on what God has done for us, rather than on what we do for Him. Whenever the emphasis is upon our works, rather than God's work, there is a tendency for authoritarian leaders to impose unbiblical burdens upon their members.

Such then are some of the basic marks of those groups we label as cults. But even in saying that, and as we shall see throughout the book, many of them are tendencies which are present in a number of more mainline churches. So there is no cause for complacency. We need to remember that many of these cults started as recognised churches. Indeed there are some groups on which, as it were, the jury is still out. Most churches, and most leaders, have within them the capability of making disastrous mistakes. Let these groups then be a lesson to us.

2
THE DECEIT OF POWER

I am a Master, come to me and drink out of me,
and you will not be thirsty, ever.

Bhagwan Shree Rajneesh

If we want to understand the phenomenon of the cult movement, we must have a grasp of their understanding and abuse of power. All cults revolve around a leader, to whom has been entrusted the secret of truth, and to whom everyone must be submissive.

In the secular world we are well aware of the deadly influence wielded by modern despots. The extraordinary hero-worship accorded to leaders in totalitarian regimes is all a part of the attempt to make people subservient to the leadership. One might look at the idolisation of such figures as Joseph Stalin or Mao Zedong to see how a vast people can be brought into submission by a cult of the leader. In *Wild Swans*, Jung Chang's fascinating account of China during the Cultural Revolution, she explains how everything in society was given over to the worship of Mao.

In school teaching stopped completely ... loudspeakers blasted out People's Daily editorials ... there was a daily column of Mao's quotations ... the slogans were engraved into the deepest folds of my brain: 'Chairman Mao is the red sun in our hearts! ... Mao Zedong Thought is our lifeline ... We will smash whoever opposes Chairman Mao ... People all over the world love our Great Leader!'

There were pages of worshipping comments from foreigners, pictures of European crowds trying to grab Mao's works.[1]

At one stage apparently 90 per cent of the literature that could be bought on the open market in Communist China was written either by or about Mao. Every true Chinese citizen had to be seen clutching his little red book, as a sign of devotion to the great leader.

The same could be said of other similar regimes. Perhaps the most oppressive in recent times has been the North Korea of Kim Il Sung. Here again the people have been forced into the most extraordinary worship of their leader. A Korean phrasebook for English speakers contains such useful expressions as,

> His Excellency Kim Il Sung is the greatest genius of present times . . . President Kim Il Sung is the sun of mankind . . . Marshal Kim Il Sung is the miracle-worker, the peerless patriot, and a giant of history.[2]

In Anthony Daniels's account of the last remaining Communist regimes, *The Wilder Shores of Marx: Journeys in a Vanishing World*, he describes one almost unbelievable scene in Department Store Number One in Pyongyang. The tourist party of which Daniels was a member was taken on a tour of the store. It was loaded with goods, and full of people milling about. Daniels took a few minutes to watch. He realised after a short time that although there were many people there nobody was actually buying anything. He tried an experiment. He approached a counter and asked to buy a pen. Chaos ensued since it seems nobody was expected to buy anything. However they eventually acceded to his request although when he got home he found the pen was totally useless!

But he carried on watching. As he did so people became nervous. Suddenly one of the people behind the counters panicked and started handing out gifts willy-nilly to the shoppers. They in turn panicked – what on earth were they to do with these gifts, all incidentally, the same? Daniels walked around the corner to find these same shoppers handing back the goods at another counter.

It was a gigantic hoax. These were not shoppers at all, but government employees, paid, at the end of each day, to play the part of shoppers, purely for the benefit of guilible Westerners. As Daniels thought about it he realised that therein lay one of the secrets of totalitarianism. If a government could persuade or bribe people into playing a game as ridiculous and humiliating as that, their control over them would be absolute. He comments:

> But this is no joke, and the humiliation it visits upon the people who take part in it, far from being a drawback, is an essential benefit to the power; for slaves who must participate in their own enslavement by signalling to others the happiness of their condition are so humiliated that they are unlikely to rebel.[3]

How terrifyingly true. Then Daniels goes on to quote some words of Vaclav Havel, which so vividly describes this process.

> Each person somehow succumbs to a profane trivialisation of his or her inherent humanity ... In everyone there is some willingness to merge with the anonymous crowd and to flow comfortably along with it down the river of pseudo-life. This is much more than a simple conflict between two identities. It is something far worse: it is a challenge to the very notion of identity itself.[4]

In many ways that is a perfect illustration of the way in which power and control is exercised within the cults. First, power is taken or claimed by an individual, justified on the basis that this is an individual uniquely set apart by God. Then that power comes to be exercised in an increasingly authoritarian way. Finally group members are brought to a point of almost total submission to the group and leader. At this point they are prepared to do almost anything for that leader, however humiliating or senseless. They become, in the process, depersonalised.

It is important to notice that it is a developing power that is exercised. If at the outset a leader claimed total allegiance, or demanded the sacrifice of members' lives, probably nobody would join up. It is the gradual increase in demands upon the member, so gradual that they do not notice, that creates the real danger. Ronald Enroth makes this telling comment in *Churches that Abuse*:

> Leaders who abuse usually develop their heavy-handed style over a period of time ... People who have been in contact with some of the pastoral leaders ... have told me that their ministry was far more benign and subdued at the beginning. Gradually, as the pastors became aware of the influence they could exert and the power they could wield, they and their ministries began to change ... they took advantage of vulnerable people, and convinced them that God had given them, the shepherds, the right to exercise authority over the flock.[5]

The Origins of Power

Let us look first then at the taking of power. Most cults begin, as we shall see, when an individual claims an authority from God himself. Apparently the leader is the recipient of some divine call setting him apart for a particular purpose. Once this divine call has been established it is not difficult to exercise power that is authoritarian in nature. After all, if this individual has received a special call from God, then he must be closer to God than anyone else. His word must be true. Hence the primary issue, as was said in the Introduction, is a theological one.

Much emphasis within the cult is therefore placed upon both the calling of the particular leader and his unique qualifications for leadership. Leaders make extravagant claims for themselves, speak glowingly of the extraordinary events that set them apart from an early age – often these accounts are simply untrue –

and generally set themselves apart as uniquely qualified for the work entrusted to them.

Consider some of the comments the Rev. Moon, founder of the Unification Church, has made about himself:

> With the fullness of time, God has sent his messenger to resolve the fundamental questions of life and the universe. His name is Sun Myung Moon ... No heroes in the past, no saints or holy men in the past, like Jesus or Confucius, have excelled us ... You may again want to ask me 'With what authority do you weigh these things?' I spoke with Jesus in the spirit world ... We are the only people who truly understand the heart of Jesus, and the hope of Jesus.[6]

Similarly Joseph Smith, founder of the Mormons, writes of his supposed call:

> I had a second vision. A personage appeared at my bedside who was glorious beyond description. He said that he was a messenger sent from the presence of God, and that his name was Moroni, that God had a work for me to do, and that my name should be had for good and evil among all nations.[7]

Others too – Charles Taze Russell (Jehovah's Witnesses), Mary Baker Eddy (Christian Science), Herbert W. Armstrong (World-wide Church of God), Bhagwan Shree Rajneesh, to name a few – have claimed a special revelation, a special anointing from God as confirmation of the truth of their ministry.

Once people have been persuaded that a certain individual has received this special call, it is only a short step before that person is accorded a respect, a devotion, indeed an infallibility that should correctly be accorded only to God Himself. Once this power is taken, it may very quickly be abused.

But before we move on we ought to look more closely at how this same sort of authority can be claimed by those within what we might regard as more orthodox churches. One such is the Boston Church of Christ, with its satellite congregations such as the London Church of Christ and the Birmingham Church of Christ (not to be confused with the mainline Churches of Christ, who have denounced them as heretical sect). They were founded in 1979 by Kip McKean, a man who had been expelled from other churches for his deceitful practices. They effectively believe that they alone are the true Christians, that nobody outside their group will be saved. They believe that a truth was divulged to Kip McKean which had been missing from the Church since around AD 350. They claim that it is only the Bible that they teach, but many other groups and churches also both believe and teach the Bible. It is therefore Kip McKean's understanding of the Bible that is authoritative, for this church. In other words, he has a knowledge of the truth withheld from any other teacher or minister. It is an outrageous claim.

In their literature Kip McKean is praised to the heavens. In an article about him in a magazine published by the church we find these remarks:

To say that Kip is a talented man is an understatement and does not do justice to him. Kip is an incredible balance of talent and is leading us because of his example in so many areas. There are brothers among us who are known for their humility, or their passion, or their creativity or their faith. Kip is leading us because he is known for all these virtues and many more. In fact, I cannot think of any virtue that Kip is not known for. There is no greater discipler, disciple, brother, husband, father, leader and friend than Kip McKean ... In reality the Boston Church of Christ happened because someone decided to walk powerfully with God. Kip, we love you, we need you, and we will continue to follow you as you follow Christ.[8]

Allowing for the hype that accompanies much talk in this church, this appears to imply that Kip McKean is so close to God, so faithful a representative, that we can leave all our thinking to him. Kip follows Christ, we will follow Kip. Therein lie the seeds of disaster. The moment you accord that sort of respect to any human teacher you give them a power that can easily be misused. They have become a mediator between us and God.

But there are many other religious leaders who look to special revelations and experiences to authenticate their ministries. There are supposed Christian leaders today who claim, among other things, that Jesus has sat in their car in a monk's habit and chatted to them; that Jesus has taken them on a personal tour of heaven and hell; that the Holy Spirit has begged them ' "for five more minutes. Just five more minutes." The Holy Spirit longed for my fellowship.'[9]

It is extraordinary just what certain teachers will teach, and what people will believe, simply because it is dressed up in language of personal revelation. Even the most obvious of nonsenses may be readily believed if it is stated with conviction by someone who has already managed to persuade their audience that they are especially close to God, and have received from God personal revelations. During one sermon broadcast to a potential audience of millions, an American evangelist made the following statement:

Man, I feel revelation knowledge already coming on me here. Lift your hands. Something new is going to happen here today. I felt it just as I walked down here . . . Hear it, hear it, hear it. See God the Father is a person, God the Son is a person, God the Holy Spirit is a person. But each one of them is a triune being by Himself. If I can shock you – and maybe I should – there's nine of them.[10]

Such talk is of course completely preposterous. But notice the incredibly subtle way in which total nonsense is dressed up to make it acceptable. 'Something new': we all love a new teaching, and are bored by what we regard as old hat. It's 'going to happen here today': we all want to be in on the action, and here the audience is told that *they* are going to be the first hearers of a unique truth. 'If I can shock you': by warning people that what they are about to hear will be shocking to many, it is as though the speaker is questioning their courage. Are you strong enough to hear this? The only correct way for anyone to react to such claptrap is to dismiss it as dangerous and baseless heresy.

We must understand how incredibly dangerous this can be. Those who can convince others of extraordinary experiences of God, are able very quickly to exercise an enormous hold upon them.

Claims of extraordinary spiritual experiences, of angelic visitations, of special divine calls, should be treated with extreme caution. All too often they are used to exert undue influence and manipulate people. But once this power has been taken, how is it used?

The Exercise of Power

We consider then the exercise of power. It needs to be said that power is not wrong in itself. No society, no organisation can exist without there being some form of authority. It is not authority that is the problem so often, but how it is exercised. Having said that, once a group has established that an individual is uniquely set apart by God, and has a unique understanding of God's ways and purposes, that individual may quickly begin to misuse that authority.

There are a number of dangers. First is that of beginning to believe one's own publicity. If enough people are convinced that one is special, unique, perfect, sooner or later that person will begin to believe it for themselves. This is of course especially true when that individual already believes himself to be set apart. This can be an almost unconscious process, even for those with the best intentions.

Paul Tournier, in his article 'The Power Abusers' wrote:

To be looked upon as a saviour leaves none of us different ... there is in us, especially in those whose intentions are of the purest, an excessive and destructive will to power which eludes even the most sincere and honest self-examination.[11]

Or, as another article in the same magazine said:

> They look on us as experts, God's mouthpieces, the interpret-
> ers of his will – to begin with for ourselves but very soon,
> before we realise it, for other people too, especially since they
> insist on requiring it of us. Very soon, too, we find ourselves
> thinking that when they follow our advice they are obeying
> God and that when they resist us they are really resisting
> God.[12]

This is one of the problems of creating any form of religious
hero. The moment a person is elevated to heroic status, they
immediately have a power and influence that can be misused.
Their opinion is sought on any number of matters – and then
quoted and requoted as being authoritative – they are asked to
speak at meetings, they are treated with a new deference. It can
be very seductive. Whenever one sees individuals' names and
pictures being splashed over the front of magazines and news-
papers, their views being sought on radio and television, particularly if they are young and inexperienced, then one is fearful.
Very soon they may begin to believe that they do have a unique
wisdom, that their views on all manner of subjects are somehow
more worth hearing that others', that they are uniquely gifted.

Second is the danger of lack of accountability. The more
important anyone becomes, the more respected, the harder it
becomes for anyone to correct them. Arrogance quickly creeps
in, and they become above contradiction. Any religious leader
who allows themselves to get into a position where there is
nobody who will tell them what is right or wrong, no one to
whom they are accountable, is in trouble. Perhaps it needs to be
somebody not too involved in the same work; often a person
will find it hard to criticise or rebuke their leader, since they
want to be 'in' with them. As H. Bussell so wisely puts it in
Unholy Devotion:

> If we are in a position over others and we fail to place
> controls on ourselves, we subtly and unknowingly start to

control others. Power that elevates a leader beyond contradiction ... will lead both the leader and the followers down a road marked by broken relationships, exploitation, and control. Power that tempers and checks itself and is wrapped in compassion is the pathway to gentleness, caring, and maturity. Jesus said, 'I am the good shepherd. The good shepherd lays down his life for the sheep' (John 10:10). He is our model of service and leadership.[13]

What is more, not only will a group not see the dangers of authoritarianism, it will even begin to make excuses for those in positions of power whom they see acting in a way that goes against their understanding of what is right. Somehow the same rules do not apply to the leadership. Members may give all their possessions and money to the group, and live in abject poverty, while their leaders swan around in the lap of luxury, yet never see any necessary contradiction.

Gary Scharff was with the Moonies for four years. In a book describing his experiences, *Suicide Training in the Moon Cult*, he talks of this double standard:

Whenever you're dealing with religious categories like resurrection and rebirth, you begin to blur your categories between life and death. When you see Moon do something that seems immoral or vulgar or crude, it's not your place to correct that. You should just accept the fact that God has chosen him. He's a perfect man. You must support him regardless of what he does.[14]

The truth is that the leader has become so powerful, and so far taken on the mantle of a god, that nobody dares criticise or question. He cannot be wrong, he must be right.

But we must also note the clear and obvious way in which some exercise this authority. In many groups there is a very tight authority structure, usually pyramidic, whereby the person at the top is able to control members at all levels. One of the most obvious methods is that of discipling or shepherding. By this each individual has another member to whom they are accountable in almost everything, and to whom anything wrong must be confessed.

Many groups practise a form of this shepherding, and it is dangerous precisely because in many ways it is so admirable. We all want others to take a personal interest in us. When they give up their time and efforts to help and encourage us it is quite flattering. But when the friendship becomes a method of manipulation and an unhealthy exercise of authority we must beware.

In some groups the relationship of a member to his discipler is the most important feature of a person's spiritual life. All teaching is somehow passed on through the discipler, all major decisions – career, place of work, choice of home or marriage partner – are made by them, and total accountability is accorded to them. It even reaches the point where the measure of a person's spiritual life is the extent of their obedience to their discipler. The Boston Church of Christ has developed this authoritarianism to an extrme degree. Here are various comments on the nature and importance of an individual's relationship to their discipler, spoken in public meetings at the church and recorded in Jerry Jones's book *What Does the Boston Church Teach?*

Often we are afraid to submit to authority because it might be abusive. Jesus was not afraid of abusive authority; he was even willing to submit and obey authority that was abusive (Phil. 2:6–11, Matt. 27:11–50) ... When we trust God we do not have to be afraid of abusive authority ... Far too many with the Church of Christ have imitated the words of Korah and other leaders of Israel who said to Moses, 'You have gone too far! The whole community is holy, everyone of them, and the Lord is with them. Why do you set yourselves above the Lord's assembly?' ... It is true that all Christians walking in the light are holy and God is indeed with everyone of them. However, it is also true that through His Spirit certain men have been assigned responsibilities to lead them in the kingdom and that to oppose them is to oppose God who anointed them.[15]

It is a sad mixture of biblical misunderstanding and emotional and spiritual blackmail. The Bible never expects or demands the sort of 'abusive authority' of which the speaker talks, within the Christian community.

But the Boston Church is not alone in this destructive form of shepherding. Among the many lessons that the Church needs to learn from the tragedy at the Nine O'Clock Service in Sheffield is the danger of over-heavy shepherding. One member summarised the way in which control was exercised in the group:

> The pastoral structure was very controlling. It was a pyramidical structure with Chris at the top, then his three closest associates and then a core leadership group of between 10 and 12 people. His right hand woman was his constant companion. We thought it was a bit odd, but we were so gullible and we presumed it was all above board.
>
> Below the leadership group were the pastoral leaders. They were chosen for their intransigence. They were a crucial part of the control structure. They trusted the people above them completely, and they thought any criticism was terrible. They were not bad people in themselves but they were trained in absolute loyalty. My pastoral leader gave me a hard time for being disobedient and critical of Chris.
>
> Below them were the group leaders. We were idealists who were trying to reconcile what was taught with what we saw happening around us. The things we taught were good and we were always trying to understand why so many people were . . . unhappy. Now I know why.[16]

On one occasion, the Rev. Moon instructed his followers: 'Father [i.e. himself] is telling you all this this morning because . . . he wants you to become a part of him, part of Sun Myung Moon . . . You are now entitled to being loved by the true

Parents by being loyal to them ... You must do anything and everything instructed by the true Parents.'[17]

What is so insidious here is the way in which the love of the 'true Parents' almost appears dependent upon their obedience. Love within the cults is indeed conditional. Do what the leaders say, and you will be loved, accepted, and honoured. Disobey, or rebel, and you become an outcast.

In addition, a true disciple is expected to obey even if they cannot understand the reasons for it. In some groups this is known as 'weird obedience', where to engage in a particular activity is somehow proof of one's devotion. One does not think, one simply obeys. Again this seems to have been the case within the Boston Church of Christ:

> A disciple is one who obeys his discipler even if he doesn't comprehend what he's told. Because he wants to have a teachable heart, he will fully obey and be totally obedient even if what he's asked to do is contrary to what he would normally do or think. To distrust the person God had put in his life is equal to distrusting God and his faith in God is shown by his faith in his discipler.[18]

Not only is this sort of teaching totally against the teaching of Scripture, particularly where the exercise of authority is concerned, it is extraordinarily unhealthy. In the same way that the submissiveness of the North Korean 'shoppers' placed them under the complete control of their leaders, so this sort of obedience removes a person's essential dignity and humanity. But of course that is the purpose. The intention of the cults is obedience, and appropriate methods are used. Whenever an individual seeks to stand against this teaching, he is invariably accused of rebelliousness, or a wrong spirit, or not being teachable.

One of the clearest signs of this sort of misuse of power is the reaction to criticism. In any group there will be those who agree with the general thrust of the movement, and those who do not, some who go along with the leadership, and others who criticise.

Criticism is in fact a healthy sign, if rightly given. Any church leader should recognise that constructive criticism is a valuable and positive thing. We may not agree with it, but we owe the individual the respect of listening to what is being said. In any case there is very little criticism from which one can learn nothing. What is more there are times when criticism has to be destructive. If an individual sees something going terribly wrong they have a duty to speak out, even at great personal cost.

Within some of these cults, however, the very act of criticism itself, from whatever source it originates, and however positively it is given, is always discouraged. Indeed it is almost invariably turned on the individual concerned. 'The problem is really with you. You are not broken enough. You have a bad attitude. You are too proud, etc.' I read recently of a group who have abused power in a frightening way, leading to tragic sexual abuse. Certain people were aware, apparently, of what was happening, but any criticism, any questioning of the leadership, led to accusations of 'not having come to terms with your own sexuality'. Criticism, however well-intentioned and wise, was always turned back upon itself.

Any leadership or any group that sets itself above criticism is inviting disaster. Where there is no internal accountability, and almost by definition for the cults there can be no external accountability, the leadership is basically freed up to do whatever it wishes. The exercise of power with no openness to correction is immensely dangerous. But even in groups where there is internal accountability the danger is not eradicated. I have heard religious leaders talk of how they are accountable to a group of elders or leaders, when in fact the group is as much implicated in their behaviour as the leader himself. When power resides within a small tightly-knit group the danger can be exacerbated.

Many years ago I recall being told by a respected Christian leader that when he analysed those people who have drifted from the Christian faith, he almost invariably noted two things. First, they had little or no sense of humour (we will return to this later), and second, they were unable to take criticism.

Perhaps the same thing could be said of those who exercise power in an authoritarian way. Any leader who cannot accept criticism is not exercising authority in the way that the New Testament at least envisages. He is merely a dictator.

The Effects of Power

But if such is the exercise of power, notice lastly the effects of power on the lives of both leader and member. We have already mentioned that the leader will often be unaware of the influence he is wielding, at least at first. Indeed one of the questions I am most often asked about cults is, 'What is the motivation of cult leaders? Are they aware of what they are doing, or are they just sincere but extremely misguided?'

The honest answer is that it is very hard to say. We do not really know what goes on within the mind of, say, a David Koresh. Those who knew him from an earlier period will say that he was always a little strange, perhaps frightening. But whether it was deliberate manipulation of people or psychological delusion is impossible to tell.

But there is a pattern within cult leaders. Maybe initially they believe they have a special message. God has called them for a special task and they must fulfil it. Maybe it is only the acclaim of others that makes them believe this. Perhaps initially they even show a genuine humility. But as time goes on they realise the power they can exert. Gradually they become intoxicated by that power. Eventually they become evil despots, too proud and self-seeking even to consider that they might be wrong. In other words what may have begun as a genuine, if misguided, desire to do what was right, in time becomes an appalling example of selfish manipulation.

In their book *Healing the Wounded*, John White and Ken Blue describe such a process:

> People who abuse power are changed progressively as they do so. In abusing power they give themselves over to evil, untruth, self-blindness, and hardness without allowing them-

selves or anyone else to see what is happening. The longer the process continues, the harder repentance becomes. Church bosses must be spotted and rescued early, or they may never be rescued at all. They have caused inconceivable havoc among churches throughout history.[19]

As time goes on they so set themselves above all other authority or correction, that they bind themselves to the evil they do. Did Jim Jones believe he was doing the right thing in causing 900 followers to commit mass suicide? Did David Koresh really believe he was the Messiah? Who can say? All we can know is that the seeds of their own destruction had been sown a long time before, when the membership abrogated the right to think.

But what of the effect on the members? When we look at the techniques used by the cults in a later chapter we will consider some of the effects, but for now it is worth noting that when individuals abdicate their power to choose for themselves, and give it to another, disaster may follow.

One of the most heart-rending stories over the last few years must have been that of Samuel Henry, a member of the Seventh Day Adventist Church in Manchester, who lost most of his closest family in the conflagration at Waco, Texas, when the Branch Davidian stronghold was stormed. In an article in the *Daily Telegraph* in January 1995, Henry spoke of the total control that Koresh exercised over his family, and his complete inability to make them see sense.

David Koresh gave them the impression that I didn't like them, saying that if I loved them I would have joined them.

They agreed with that. They were so brainwashed that anything he told them, they believed. Diana [his eldest daughter] thought he was a prophet and a great man of God. But this man was demon-possessed.

All they talked about was the Word. They stopped praying because they were told by David Koresh that they were not holy enough to pray to God. He was the Messiah and as long as they were with him, they were all right.[20]

With what tragic consequences!

In its most extreme form, cult control leads to a diminution of personality. The individual is no longer able to make independent decisions. Everything has been decided for them for so long that their own ability to decide has been eroded. Often the sense of humour is gone, to be replaced by a faraway expression, and inability to concentrate. Without the leader and the group all else seems empty and meaningless. Whereas a true faith should enable a character to blossom, in the cults the personality is almost invariably repressed. It is inevitable. Individuality or nonconformity is frowned upon. It makes control so much harder.

Herein lies an enormous challenge for conventional churches, in many of which today there is a greater exercise of authority, tending towards authoritarianism. Widely respected Christian groups have been split apart over the issue of authority. This has happened in a number of charismatic churches, and the reason is not hard to see. Where the authority is seen to reside not in the Bible but rather in the individual revelations given to certain people, the implication is that they must be nearer God than others. Their revelations are therefore accorded greater respect than the teaching of the Bible. They take upon themselves the right to impose their authority, or at least demand respect.

Some even set themselves up as latter-day apostles. I will never forget the sight of one British Christian leader, in an interview on television, comparing himself to the early Apostles. He was asked if he called himself an apostle. He replied that he was sure Paul never called himself Apostle Paul, simply Paul. Similarly Peter was just Peter, not Apostle Peter. So he did not call himself Apostle X, simply X. What was so frightening was that he was appearing to elevate himself to the level of the biblical apostles, as though he was an equal, and that what had been true of them was true of him. It would therefore be natural to claim for himself the power and authority of an Apostle. It was an incredibly dangerous road down which he was beginning to travel. It is a warning to many today.

3

THE DISTORTION OF TRUTH

What do they teach?

'The world belongs to those who offer it hope.'
Teilhard de Chardin

It used to be said of the Athenians of New Testament times that they loved something new. 'All the Athenians and the foreigners who lived there spent their time doing nothing but talking about and listening to the latest ideas' (Acts 17:21). But it was not a characteristic confined to them – it also seems to be a characteristic of our culture today. Human beings by nature are conservative animals, loving the tried and tested and suspicious of the new. Tradition is an important stabilising factor in society. Today, however, we appear different. We love new ideas and new philosophies. We love to impress our friends with new thinking they have not heard of before. We love to be trendy.

When one considers for a moment that people who reject the Christian faith out of hand will readily embrace New Age thinking, or teaching that Christ was really an astronaut, as in the teaching of Erik von Daniken, one realises that it is usually not the truth of a philosophy that matters, but its novelty.

In the early Church there was a group of religious teachers who came to be known as Gnostics. While we need not dwell on the actual teachings they embraced – indeed there was a wide variety in those teachings – their attraction lay in the fact that what they propagated was something special and different.

They had discovered a new knowledge (gnosis) that alone offered the true or complete salvation.

It was, of course, attractive. It did not try to deny Christianity as such – although some of the teachings ran directly counter to orthodox Christianity – rather it argued that biblical Christianity did not go quite far enough. Some extra teaching, revelation or experience was needed. It was perhaps against an early form of Gnosticism that much of the teaching of the New Testament was directed. The sad thing is that today this same obsession with new ideas is again leading many people astray.

It is difficult in some ways to speak generally about the teachings of the cults since they are so many and varied. There are as many different teachings as there are different teachers. Again, often it is not the teaching that really matters; in most cases it is submission to the leadership that is the key. What this tends to mean is that there is within many of the cults a deep distrust of the mind. A member is not encouraged to think independently, rather to receive whatever the leader passes on. An obvious example of this is the teaching of Bhagwan Shree Ranjneesh: 'It is not that the intellect sometimes misunderstands. Rather, the intellect always misunderstands. It is not that the intellect sometimes errs; it is that the intellect is the error. It always errs.'[1]

If there is this inherent mistrust of the mind we would be unwise to expect a clear, coherent body of teaching. The only thing that really matters is whether the member is subservient – not just to the teaching, but more importantly to the leadership. This explains why it is that groups can often change their teaching quite radically, or even hold beliefs that are directly contradictory, without members seeming either to notice or object. Theirs is not to reason why, only to submit. However there are traits that they have in common, and I will point out three areas of concern.

The Basis of Heresy

The first is the area of origin. Where do these teachings come from? If you look closely you will see that almost all of the cults or new religious movements begin with an individual, who claims some special revelation from God. It may be in a dream, or vision, but in some way God communicates His truth to this person uniquely. They then gather around them a group of people convinced that this person is possessed of exceptional powers and wisdom, and very soon a cult develops.

An obvious example would be that of Joseph Smith, founder of the Mormons, otherwise known as the Prophet. Born in Vermont in 1805, son of a man who spent most of his time digging for imaginary treasures and making counterfeit money, Smith claimed to have received the first of his visions in 1820. This informed him that God was not best pleased with the efforts of the Christian Church and that he, Smith, had been chosen to launch a restoration of true Christianity. In 1823 the angel Moroni allegedly appeared to him, and that saw the beginning of Smith's relationship to the 'golden plates' that would form the Book of Mormon. This revelation was duly recorded in the Pearl of Great Price. Numerous other visions, revelations, and discoveries took place as the Mormon religion was founded.

It is important to note that Joseph Smith did not see his religion as contradicting the Christianity of his background, rather as restoring it. The true faith had been lost, but was recovered with the new revelation given to him. Mormons theoretically do not deny the teaching of the Bible, but its authority has been superseded by the teaching of the Book of Mormon, Pearl of Great Price, and Doctrine and Covenants. Indeed Mormons have developed a clever escape clause for teaching that the Bible is not to be trusted completely. The Bible, for a Mormon, is authoritative in so far as it is 'translated correctly'. Effectively that means that wherever the Bible disagrees with their teaching, it is the Bible that is wrong, or has been translated incorrectly. Incidentally, it is interesting to note that the Book of Mormon, which they also claim to be the Word of God, and their most authoritative guide, has actually undergone something over three thousand revisions since it was first published.

In other words, what we have here is a new teaching, a new revelation, entrusted to one person at a particular moment, a revelation that transcends all other revelations and is uniquely authoritative. It is this revelation that sets this group apart, and make them bearers of the only truth. Others may have some of the truth, but they alone have its fullness.

Look at any other cult and you will probably find almost exactly the same pattern. An individual, often a little strange with an odd background, and dissatisfied with ordinary religion, receives direct from God a new and special message. From this moment this person is God's special mediator, the one entrusted with God's truth, the one infallible teacher.

Charles Taze Russell, founder of the Jehovah's Witnesses, makes exactly this same claim for himself and his teaching. The Bible cannot be understood unless he, Russell, interprets it (through his 'Scripture Studies'). Without his interpretation a person is bound to get it wrong:

> If anyone lays the 'Scripture Studies' aside . . . and goes to the Bible alone, although he has understood his Bible for ten years, our experience shows that within two years he goes into darkness. On the other hand, if he had merely read the 'Scripture Studies' with their references and had not read a page of the Bible as such, he would be in the light at the end of two years, because he would have the light of the Scriptures.[2]

Although Russell pays lip-service to the teaching of the Bible it is clear that he regards the Bible as a lesser revelation to the one that he has received, or at least as subservient to his interpretation. Herein lies an important principle. Whenever any person or group claims that they are the sole true interpreters of the Bible, the authority has effectively passed from the Bible to them. This elevation of a particular interpretation is often quite unconscious. It just becomes a sort of theological filter through which everything is viewed.

This is exactly what we find with the Rev. Sun Myung Moon,

founder of the Moonies. He teaches that Jesus Christ was a failure, since he should have come to have the perfect family, and was thwarted by his death, which was a mistake – despite all the New Testament evidence that states that Jesus came to die. The Rev. Moon claims to have been given the unique task of putting things right. Where Jesus failed, he, the Rev. Moon, will succeed. Thus the age of Christianity is over, to be succeeded by the age of Moon: 'God is now throwing Christianity away and is establishing a new religion, and this new religion is the Unification Church ... With the fullness of time, God has sent his messenger to resolve the fundamental questions of life and universe. His name is Sun Myung Moon.'[3]

Paul Wierwille of The Way International speaks in a similar fashion when he explains how he came to understand the truth as it was specially revealed to him. 'I was praying ... and that's when He spoke to me audibly, just like I'm talking to you now. He said He would teach me the Word as it has not been known since the first century if I would teach it to others.'[4]

Another group leader justifies his particular teaching like this: 'God let me know that no man had entered that highest realm that I saw. He allowed me to experience things that no man had ever seen. I was connected with God; I had reveleation, I was one with Jesus Christ.'[5]

How often one hears individuals introducing some new teaching, often horrifyingly far from orthodoxy, with similar words: 'God revealed this truth to me'.

It need hardly be stated how dangerous this can be. New revelations, by definition, cannot be tested, because they go beyond what has been understood or revealed before. One can only accept or reject them. They apply an appalling emotional and spiritual pressure upon others. The implication is always, if you do not accept this teaching then you are rejecting God. To stand against the leader is to rebel against God because that leader is the true mediator of God's truth.

Any group that effectively claims that only they are right is really falling into this trap of a latter-day gnosticism, claiming a new revelation which alone will save. One of the most active groups in London do just that. They claim to be orthodox Christians, and believe the Bible. But they do not have a basis of faith – the only basis they claim to need is the Bible. However, although this position may seem admirable, deeper inspection reveals it to be very disturbing.

There are many groups that claim the Bible as their supreme authority. It is the classic Christian position, with the Bible as supreme rule and authority. But no other group interprets the Bible in precisely the way that this group does. In essence, therefore, this group judges others, and indeed disqualifies them, not on the basis of whether they believe the Bible, but whether they believe their understanding of the Bible, which is of course very different. In fact it is even more disturbing than that because their understanding derives solely from the teaching of their leader. In other words they believe that their leader is the only true interpreter of the Bible today, his teaching the only true teaching.

But what is at issue here? It is not just a question of interpretation. Is my interpretation more correct than yours? It runs deeper than that. What is at issue here is not the authority of the Bible, but of particular teachers of the Bible. In claiming that one person is the only faithful interpreter of the Bible – as many of these groups do – they have taken the authority away from the Bible, and placed it in an individual. They are in effect claiming that the Bible is only authoritative in so far as it is interpreted by a particular individual.

Surely this is no less than latter-day gnosticism, where one person claims to have the unique revelation of truth. It is of course cloaked in a Christian veneer, but is no less dangerous for all that.

There are numerous other examples where so-called Christian leaders begin to take upon themselves the mantle of prophet or mediator and their word is taken as gospel. We will look more closely at this when we consider the exercise of authority within these groups, but at this point one need only say this. Where the leaders are held in exceptional respect, and their teaching regarded as the true teaching, it is only a short step before they are able to propagate quite outrageous ideas without anyone standing against them.

Here in London we recently witnessed a series of meetings led by a well-known evangelist. This man claims that at the age of fourteen God showed him something of the ministry he was to exercise. He became, in his words, a 'mouthpiece for God', capable of 'revealing things which had not yet come to pass, precisely communicating direct "Thus saith the Lord" words from God'. Some of the teachings he has embraced have been directly contradictory to orthodox Christian teaching, but because he claims to have had this revelation it is not easy to stand against him.

One first therefore needs to look at the origins of any teaching to see if it is in accord with traditional orthodoxy. Where it depends on any new revelation there is reason to be extremely sceptical. As an American Christian once wisely commented, 'If it's new, it ain't true. If it's true, it ain't new.'

Neither must we be fooled by those who claim historical orthodoxy for their beliefs. Each creed, each religion needs one supreme authority, indeed it can only have one. Christians believe in the authority of the Bible, the Church (through its teaching) and reason. All three are needed to understand correctly. But of these three only one can be the supreme authority. If for instance the Bible teaches one thing, a particular church teaches another, and my reason suggests something else, which am I to believe? Only one of these three can be supremely authoritative, and the historic answer of the Christian Church has been the Bible.

Within many of these religious cults there is a stated acceptance of the authority of the Bible. But it is not *supremely* authoritative. The Mormons may claim that they accept the authority of the Bible in so far as it is 'translated correctly', but they still teach doctrines that run directly contrary to the teaching of the Bible. 'As we are, God was. As God is, we shall become.' Such is foundational Mormon teaching, but it is totally against the teaching of the Bible. The Bible is not supremely authoritative because they teach doctrine contrary to it.

The Moonies may claim, as one did to me one day outside Safeways, that the Rev. Moon's teaching is not against the Bible, but just contains a deeper truth (beware the word 'deeper' – it almost invariably spells trouble). But they still insist that the mission of Jesus was a failure, because he did not come to die, despite the fact that the Bible states on innumerable occasions that his death was the reason above all that Jesus did come.

Important questions to ask, therefore, when trying to ascertain of a particular group whether it is orthodox, might be: what is the source of their teaching? Where do their teachings come from? What is their supreme authority? Have the teachers of that group been elevated to a point that whatever they say, regardless of whether there is external authority for it or not, is accepted within the group? When that becomes the case we must beware.

The Content of Heresy

The second area to look at is the content of the teaching. As I said earlier, it is hard to summarise teaching that is so diverse, but within the religious cults, particularly those that have sprung up within the Christian tradition, there are common denominators.

The first is seen in their attitude to moral or religious law, which is marked by *legalism*, or its complete opposite, *antinomianism*. By legalism I mean a commitment to a set of rules, in the keeping of which there is true salvation. It may be a religious legalism – the keeping of particular festivals, religious duties, ceremonies, etc. It may be a moral legalism – obedience to a strict moral code of behaviour. But behind many of the cults you will find some form of legalism, the idea that salvation is to be gained through the keeping of these rules, through this form of behaviour.

By antinomianism I mean a total freedom from rules, indeed a license to act in whatever way one wishes – this often means some form of sexual license. The strange thing is that some groups can be both legalistic and antinomian at the same time – legalistic in religious observance, antinomian in behaviour.

One of the great features of the teaching of Christ is the idea that it is not what a person does that will ultimately save him. After all, none of us is or ever will be good enough for God. Instead salvation is a free gift of God which an individual chooses to accept or reject. It can never be earned.

But the human tendency is frequently to revert to a form of legalism. We all want to be told what we can do. So from the earliest days of the church teachers have been telling us that there is something we must do, in addition to the offer God makes us. In other words, legalism always creeps in.

A very active group in the UK at present fall into precisely this trap. They teach that while salvation is by faith, it is not by faith alone. It is by faith *and* works. It is not enough to trust God, you also have to evangelise – indeed two years ago four hundred members of the church were excommunicated because they were not reckoned to be evangelising enough – and be baptised by them (nobody else's baptism is good enough, I fear). But how can you know if you have done enough evangelising? What happens if you have a bad week? or a bad month? Well, there's the rub. Only your discipler can really tell if you have done enough, and have made it. Do you see therefore how this form of salvation by works becomes an abominable slavery? You never really know if you have done enough, and are pathetically dependent on your discipler to reassure you. Indeed it can be used as a sanction upon you. If you even so much as question your discipler this represents a bad attitude and can threaten your salvation. Result? You toe the line, and do your best to please.

I think of a conversation I had with a Jehovah's Witness some time ago. He was telling me how they were expected to spend up to twenty hours a week visiting. It was through this sort of good work that he was hoping to be saved. The trouble was, as he admitted to me, he was not a particularly faithful or obedient Witness. So I asked him how he could know he was 'saved'. He had no answer. For him the idea that one could ever be confident of pleasing God was an alien one. But of course it was. If our being acceptable to God is dependent upon our works we will almost never know when or if we have done enough.

Notice too how legalism becomes a means of oppression and manipulation. The moment we buy into the idea that by doing something we might be acceptable to God is the moment we hand over the responsibility for that decision to another human being. We invest them with the power to determine whether we have done enough. And we will do anything to please them if it means they will give us that reassurance.

But strangely, as already intimated, these groups are sometimes extremely antinomian in behaviour, and we will cover this in more detail in a later chapter.

So legalism is often the first mark of this teaching – it tells us there is something we must *do*. The second is *subjectivism*. This tells us there is something we must *experience*. In one sense this is contradictory – you cannot really teach an experience. But what is alarming about many of these groups is the almost total subjectivity of them. It is not so much what is taught that really matters, as the *feel* of everything.

I spoke recently with a member of the Church of Scientology. I asked him what the church actually stood for and believed. He was unable to answer. You may have seen the endless stickers or flyers advertising the benefits of Dianetics, the technique developed by L. Ron Hubbard, founder of the movement – you will have done if you live anywhere near central London. They are full of the benefits of Dianetics, how it will solve your problems, how it will solve the world's problems. But they will not tell you what this Dianetics actually is. The point is that it is incredibly hard to work out. Essentially it seems to be some form of self-analysis, of looking inward at the self, which will have a beneficial effect on the rest of life. This analysis relies heavily upon the authority of an auditor, which means it becomes a form of manipulation.

But it is there with more orthodox seeming groups – the idea that you have to have a particular experience to be one of the few. It is one of the problems of the modern church that so often we are judged by our experience. Do we speak in tongues? Have we had the blessing? Indeed what is taught is that it is more important to have the blessing than believe some teaching.

What this leads to is an experience-centred Christianity or religion where what is experienced is everything, and what is believed is of little account. It is perhaps of little surprise that the Nine O'Clock Service in Sheffield had aligned itself with a theology that it would originally have shunned, because it became far more about an experience, and far less about a particular creed. One of its members expressed its aim: 'It is designed to be a place where beat, mediation, dance and light can reconnect people with God, transforming their vision of the world.'6

How are people reconnected with God? Not seemingly through a particular belief, but through an experience. The difficulty with this is that it gives us almost no criteria by which to judge any experience. If someone claims that through doing something, however bizarre, they have an experience 'of God', they cannot be refuted. Subjectivism, which is really existentialism, is a dangerous route.

The third feature is *dualism*. Classically dualism is a belief that sets God against Satan as two warring powers, almost equal in authority. The world is thus seen as the ground upon which this cosmic battle is taking place. At one moment God seems to be winning, at another, the devil. Of course this is a gross misunderstanding of biblical teaching on spiritual warfare. In this there is no question who is the ultimate authority – God – nor that Satan will ultimately be vanquished for ever. Nevertheless in our world Satan still exercises some power.

In many of the cults this teaching about good and evil is greatly distorted. The members see themselves as the forces for good in the world – servants of God. Anyone who opposes them is seen as a servant of Satan, or as a force for evil. Everything is either black or white, good or evil, every person a servant of God or a servant of Satan. To use the words of Jesus, albeit in a totally different context, he who is not with them is against them.

Of course this is an extremely useful belief for these groups to hold, because it sets them apart from any criticism anyone might make of them. Since they and they alone are the servants of God, and anyone else is a messenger of Satan, they cannot and must not listen to anyone else, all outside criticism is invalid, and in a sense they are safe. It becomes a self-contained community and ideology.

This explains how so many of these groups are able to cut themselves off from family, friends, and society as a whole. Since everyone else is an enemy, working for Satan, they must be contaminated by them as little as possible. It explains why one of the first marks of cultist practice and behaviour will always be a withdrawal from normal activities of life, and from normal spheres of living. It explains why many cult members will not listen to anyone outside the group. They have been persuaded that anyone outside the group is working for the enemy. Therefore they must not listen to them, indeed should break off contacts with them. Such behaviour is often seen as a test of loyalty.

Often the enemy is seen as the government. The government is the Big Brother waiting to pounce, never to be trusted, the agent of evil. Indeed within the cults conspiracy theories abound. L. Ron Hubbard, founder of the Church of Scientology, said this:

> The mighty Interpol, that tool of the CIA has been found to be a nest of war criminals hiding out from the Law itself [although] you do not hear much about this from the running dog press because of course they were the tool of the enemy in the first place.
>
> All you have to do is to count the memberships of the churches. And you know conclusively that while the enemy goes down, whatever the bombast, Scientology is going up.[7]

Again, it suits such groups to paint the government as the enemy. It helps explain why they might not always pay taxes, why they evoke the government's hostility, why government laws and rules do not have to be abided by.

It is an important feature of cults that they form this self-contained ideology, where everything has its own explanation. While someone is in the cult it all makes perfect sense. Why do so many oppose them? Because they are working for the devil. Why does the government try to extort money from them? Because they are evil. Why are the groups so often accused of brainwashing, mind-control, etc.? Because the enemy will look for anything to throw at the group. A group member will never look at the truth of these allegations because they are convinced that they are coming from a servant of evil. As such they can contain no truth.

Notice where this form of dualism leads. The fourth feature of cultic teaching is *apocalypticism*. By this I mean that the world is presented as heading towards this enormous showdown between good and evil, where the group's loyalty will be tested to the limit. We will think later in the book about the appalling denouements at Jonestown and Waco, but we need to see that cult teaching has often inevitably led in that direction. If life is seen as this dualistic confrontation between good and evil, God and Satan, it is almost inevitable that there will be a final conflagration.

So much teaching is taken up with references, often oblique, to the final test that is coming. Members are questioned about their commitment – will they be prepared for what is going to happen? Will they be able to stand firm? Of course it is all very subtle, but there is this undercurrent.

In the aftermath of the bomb in Oklahoma City, one of the most disturbing things to come out was the existence of far-right groups, who claimed a religious zealotry, hated the government and were expecting and preparing for a military outcome. The *Daily Telegraph* quoted some of their leaders:

Nor ... is there considered to be a contradiction between God and guns. Albert Esposito, leader of one of the militia groups in North Carolina, urges his members to prepare for the coming confrontation by accumulating caches of the 'four Bs – bibles, bullets, beans, and bandages.'

Rev Norman Olson, commander of the Michigan Militia, which is the largest and best-organised in the country, doubles up as a Baptist preacher and a gun dealer. He gives the same advice to his congregation as to his customers: 'We're talking about a situation where armed conflict may be inevitable if the country doesn't turn around.'[8]

We have seen exactly the same with the terrifying followers of the Aum Shinri Kyo (Supreme Truth) sect in Japan. They are reported to have stockpiled enough lethal chemicals to kill up to ten million people, or make lots of toothpaste and fertiliser. Their leader is Shoko Asahara, who for many has taken on the status of a Messiah figure. They have an estimated thirty thousand followers in Russia. In a recent attack on the Tokyo Underground believed to be caused by the group, ten people were killed and around five thousand injured.

They too have an apocalyptic vision. They believe that final war will erupt in 1997 between Japan and America, laying waste twentieth century civilisation. A member was quoted in an article in the *Observer*:

There was so much pollution, environmental destruction and disease. I felt as though I was being eaten away. But when I read Master Asahara's books, I began to understand about life and death and reincarnation ... I am still at an early stage but I am beginning to achieve emancipation. I sleep only three hours a night and devote my waking hours to Master Asahara's teaching.[9]

This apocalyptic theme is prevalent in many of these groups and, as we shall see, it is both attractive and deadly.

The Development of Teaching

Third, we notice the development of teaching. Sometimes a group will teach something that is so blatantly untrue or dangerous that they then change it, or at least play it down, to avoid bad publicity. An obvious example of this would be those groups which have foretold the end of the world on certain dates. When the dates have duly passed and the end of the world has not taken place you would expect the group to become somewhat disillusioned. This rarely takes place, however,. Usually some explanation is found for God changing his mind, or some different interpretation is placed upon the original prophecy.

Charles Russell prophesied that the parousia (commonly understood as the return of Christ) would take place in 1914. The event did not take place. So now we learn from Jehovah's Witnesses that the word parousia does not actually mean 'coming' but 'presence', and that Christ has been present in the world since 1914, but in a hidden way: 'Christ has turned his attention toward earth's affairs and is dividing the peoples and educating the true Christians [the Witnesses] in preparation for their survival during the great storm of Armageddon . . .'[10]

Some years ago I heard a radio interview with the leader of a group which had taught that Christ would return in 1951. He was quite unperturbed by the fact that this had not happened, and baldly stated that in fact Christ had started to plan his return in 1951. As they say, if you will believe that . . .

It is a lesson, however, that the Church needs to learn. There is a strong tendency within Christian circles to speak of future events, and make bold predictions. When these do not take place, there is always some excuse. Some years ago in London the church was informed that revival would come in October 1990. We waited, and some meetings were even planned at which the revival was meant to begin. But nothing untoward appeared to happen. Immediately the damage limitation started. Some claimed that in fact revival had never been predicted in the first place. Others said that God withheld his blessing because the church was not ready for it, that it was somehow the church's fault. Still another wrote a letter to the Christian press to ask 'What is revival if not 5,000 people gathered at a meeting in Docklands?'

It is the same principle. When we believe one thing, and facts arise which directly contradict that belief, we have a way of subtly altering the belief to accommodate the facts. It is not just the cults that do this. We see it in Christian circles – on occasions I have been guilty of it – and we need to be very careful because it can lead to all sorts of difficulties.

So although there are many dissimilarities between the various groups in terms of what is taught, there are also striking similarities. They seem to stem from this idea of a new revelation. They teach legalism/antinomianism, subjectivism, dualism, and have an over-detailed, speculative, apocalyptic vision of the end. And the beliefs are always subject to change.

Sadly, much of this could equally be said of supposed Christian churches. How often they look for new revelations, which always seem to be seen as more important than the old truths. Some churches even make a distinction – not to be found anywhere in the Bible – between the Logos, or timeless word, and the Rhema, or word for today. I fear that when that is done the door is opened to all sorts of dangerous and strange ideas.

Within churches too we often find elements of legalism, subjectivism, dualism, and apocalypticism. It is much easier to be told what to do, or be encouraged to have a particular experience, than it is to hold on in trust to the mercy of God. People want proof or reassurance so often that they are wide open to those who peddle a false assurance. People love to talk in apocalyptic terms, and see themselves as the central figures in an enormous spiritual battle – it appeals to a sense of the dramatic.

Some Christians are also often guilty of adapting beliefs to fit the prevailing moods. They can be all too like the 'infants' of whom Paul speaks in Ephesians 4:14 who are 'tossed back and forth by the waves, and blown here and there by every wind of teaching and by the cunning and craftiness of men in their deceitful scheming.' Lacking the theological or biblical framework for making wise judgments or discerning dubious teaching, they chase after every attractive new revelation.

4

THE DECEPTION
OF INNOCENTS

Who are the victims?

*'The issue is not whether religious sentiment is true,
but whether religious feelings are useful.'*
Dr Carl Henry

'I was doing well in my studies and having a great time
socially at University, but like many people, I was searching
for some sort of spiritual reality in my life. Towards the end
of my first year, a friend – a bright, attractive and friendly
person – invited me to his church for a Sunday service. I
thought I would go, as I fancied myself as being open and
experimental. After the service, he suggested we study the
Bible together, and I then met with him regularly, as well as
going to the Church on Sundays and to other midweek
meetings. The people impressed me with their strict sense of
morality, conviction about the Bible and their commitment.
It was challenging to my own habits and ideas.

'Although other people had warned me about the strict
"fundamentalism" of this group, and that it was rumoured to
be a cult, my friend was urgent and insistent about our
meeting together to study, and so I continued to meet with
him. He showed me such care and love that it was hard to
say no.

'Eventually, because I became convinced that the teachings
were true, I was baptised and became a member. For months
I kept the baptism a secret from my family.'

This is the story of one young student who became caught up in the London Church of Christ, and it highlights an important point. It is a common misconception that members of the cults are weak, vulnerable, and gullible, easy prey for those trying to recruit them: a few promises of truth, some open displays of affection, and a clear sense of direction are often all that is needed to bring them in, so the argument goes. But this tends to fly in the face of the evidence. On the whole the cults do not aim for the weak, or disadvantaged in society – indeed such people would often not be welcome at all. In fact the most common recruit will be above average intelligence, young, idealistic, with a clear sense of moral duty and perhaps a certain disillusionment with recognised authority.

This is why so many of the cults aim for students and concentrate in areas of high student population. One particularly aggressive group speaks of student work as 'the goose that laid the golden egg'. They see how work among students moves faster and can pay longer term dividends than any other. Students tend not to have decided what to do with their lives, have fewer family ties than others, and more time on their hands. They make ideal cult material. This is particularly so when they may be students living in a foreign country, without many friends or commitments.

A report for the European Community makes this clear:

It is the young who appear most attracted. The prime ages appear to be 18–25, with a heavy concentration of recruits among those who are entering their middle and later years at university. Most come from stable families of traditional background, where there is generally an acceptance of Christian belief of some kind. There rarely seem to be financial or marital problems within the family. Most recruits appear to demonstrate a healthy idealism naturally common to the young and a willingness to consider and discuss new ideas. There is a general sense of doubt regarding established and traditional approaches to political and social problems. Many have begun to ponder seriously their own futures in a world which seems increasingly less secure.[1]

It should also be said that there is much debate as to whether we can actually call such people victims. Excepting those appalling cases where there is irrefutable evidence of child abuse, for the most part the 'victims' are adults who are perfectly able to make up their minds for themselves. We may not always applaud or agree with others' decisions, but in this society at least we seek to defend their right to make them. There have been recent court cases where new religious movements have argued very forcefully that their members are free agents, and have made willing choices to join, and should not in any way be forced to leave. They are, to coin a phrase, consenting adults.

But what is it that makes certain people vulnerable? Why should normal, above-average intelligence, rational people fall for ideas and teachings that in their more lucid moments they would recognise as being fraudulent? After all, most young people would be mortified to think that they might fall for a particular cult – it only happens to other people.

In his book *Combating Cult and Mind Control*, Steven Hassan mentions three important factors. The first is 'the age-old philosophical notion' that man is a rational being. As such we are responsible for and in control of every action that we take. Thus an individual will only get involved in a cult if they willingly choose to. The unfortunate thing is that as human beings we are not totally rational beings. We do not always choose the wisest or the best course, even when we know what it is. The Roman poet Ovid summed up this dilemma when he wrote, 'We know and approve the better, yet do the worse.' We do not always act in a rational way. Our emotions often lead us in a different direction.

Equally this denies the effect that certain physical conditions can have upon us. Lack of sleep, peer pressure, a restricted diet have caused people to act in a way they would not otherwise have done. Whatever we like to think, we are not merely rational animals.

The second factor is a belief in our own invulnerability. We like to think that others might be susceptible, but we would not. Wanting control over our own lives, we cannot believe that someone or something else could take us over. So when we hear of others falling for a cult we are apt to blame it on them. They are weak, vulnerable, obvious targets, unable to cope with life as it is.

But although there are a number who are caught at a low point in their lives, many get involved in a cult without looking for it, or feeling a need for it at all. In fact this belief in our own invulnerability can leave us more open to being recruited, something cult members will play on. 'Now, John,' they may say, 'you look like someone who knows his own mind, you would not fall for anything. You will not let some crazy group brainwash you. Come along and decide for yourself.' By such flattery many have become involved.

The third factor is the idea that everything is mind-control anyway. We are constantly being influenced by other forces, so why worry about it? A cult can no more control or take us over than the television. Of course there is force in the argument. But what matters is if some technique is used to change our whole way of thinking without our informed consent, making us more dependent on an outside force.

Having said all that, there are common features in those who get involved. So perhaps the best way to understand the phenomenon is to recognise that cults very often meet particular needs.

The Search for Transcendence

As a whole, society has largely abandoned a belief in traditional Christian faith. It is regarded by many as irrational, outdated, and irrelevant. While traditional faith may have been rejected, however, nothing has been able to take its place. It is a source of continual frustration to many secular humanists that there still exists this desire to believe in something other than or outside of ourselves. Somehow a purely rationalist view of the world does not meet this desire for transcendence.

There is a desperate hunger for experience. Hence the appeal of much Eastern philosophy and religion which promises out-of-body experiences, deep peace, and greater fulfilment. Perhaps too it is a desire which finds expression for some in certain mind-controlling drugs. The appeal of other-worldly experiences and mystical feelings is very powerful.

This desire for an experience of the transcendent has been well described by David Wells in his book *God in the Wasteland* in speaking of the baby-boomer generation (those born in the late 1950s and 1960s).

Among the boomers inside and outside the church, two traits are most evident. First, there is a hunger for religious experience but an aversion to theological definition of that experience. And their characteristic abandonment of boundaries – between God and the self and between one religion and another – typically results in a smorgasbord of spirituality for which the only accepted criterion of truth is the pragmatic one of what seems to work personally. This is connected to the second trait, which is that baby boomers are inveterate shoppers ... This generation is in the market for religious goods and it is only to be expected that one person's purchase will be different from another person's, because every person is different, with special needs.[2]

In other words, what Wells notes is that there is a hunger for experience, wherever that may come from. It is not truth that matters but experience. Indeed experience for many is the only real arbiter of truth. Thus we can shop for whatever religion we want, wherever we want, without worrying whether something is true or not.

This explains the intense excitement about anything that smacks of the supernatural. Not long ago there was much in the news about the idols in various Hindu temples, both in the UK and India, drinking milk given them by devotees. It is hard to see why this should excite such enthusiasm other than the eternal quest for the transcendent. It is perhaps the same desire which prompts such excitement at every supposed apparition of the Virgin Mary, or at the outbreak of wild manifestations at certain charismatic services. This is not to deny their reality, or downplay their importance, but simply to state the obvious – that as human beings we have a fascination for the supernatural and transcendent. It is a fascination the cults often play upon. Anyone who has seen film of the spiritual manifestations apparent at meetings run by Bhagwan Shree Rajneesh will know both the weirdness and the lure of such things.

But it does of course make analysing, or even criticising the cults very difficult. Once one has bought into that line of thinking it is very hard to attack anyone else's point of view. An article in the *Observer* put the point very clearly: 'The bottom line for the most broad-minded liberals is whether the customer is satisfied. If a person experiences a genuine and lasting feeling of enhanced worth as a result of joining a cult, then doesn't that validate the existence of that cult?'[3]

The Search for Authority

In a recent survey in Canada conducted among young people, the most common answer to the question, 'What do you wish for most in life?' was 'Somebody we can trust'. It seems that the enormous dissatisfaction with the solutions offered by the government, society, or the Church is matched only by the desire for something else to fit into the vacuum. Those traditional bastions of authority can no longer be trusted, but we need something or someone else.

As a society we may well have dispensed with traditional morality, but it has left a vacuum, and one that is acutely felt by many. In an earlier generation, it may well have been the case that children were embarrassed by the conservatism of their parents, and parents by the liberalism of their children. In some parts of society today, however, the situation has been reversed, and now it is the parents who are shocked by their children's conservatism, and children by their parents' liberalism.

Young people need clear boundaries, a genuine sense of what is right and wrong. Without it they flounder. Yet one of the saddest results of the liberalism of the 1960s is that today's parents have lost all confidence to say what is right and wrong. Consequently their children, unable to find moral authority at home, seek it elsewhere, or at least respond to it when they find it.

Donald Taylor, professor of Psychology at McGill University, made this interesting comment.

Cults ... are increasingly attractive and influential because life is more fragmented and confusing. The standards that used to be set by parents, school and church are breaking down. We don't have the same guide-rails. We all need a coherent structure ... Cults can do that. They appeal not only to the vulnerable – the bereaved, divorced and lonely – but to those who sense a malady in society.

A charismatic cult leader tells people he understands their concerns. He offers a refuge, something that makes sense of existence, something satisfyingly different. Cult members support each other and have a sense of being an elite. A cult becomes its own world in which, to its adherents, the extreme and the bizarre may seem perfectly normal and rational.[4]

I have no desire to endorse the authoritarianism of the cults, nor the use of manipulation. But it is unquestionably true that for many the moral certainty they offer is a refreshing change from a sea of liberalist thinking that makes no moral judgments and offers no moral guidelines. The cults are only stepping in where society's traditional standard-bearers of morality have failed.

The Search for Certainty

Along with this desire to find an authority to respect and respond to there lies a deep desire for certainty, to know things for sure. This is not to be confused with a search for truth, indeed the search for truth is often subsumed in this other search. We want certainty without proof, knowledge without thought. It is a sad feature of today's world that it has largely ceased to think. We are dominated by the television. The average young person spends in excess of twenty hours a week watching television, so it is likely to have an enormous influence on the way in which they think. So many of our ideas, beliefs, and philosophies are formed not by our own thinking but by the makers of television programmes.

Equally the world is a frightening place. Wars break out all over the world; the moment one ceases another starts. Man's inhumanity to man has never been more clearly or horrifyingly documented. We long therefore for a strong, moral lead, and some certainty amid the confusion.

What the cults offer may well be simplistic solutions, dangerous half-truths, and ignorant declarations, but at least there is a ring of authority to them, and they take our concerns seriously. In many ways they remove from us the need to think, they promise us that this or that leader is the wisest of all and has done the thinking for us, and we can be certain of their wisdom. Indeed, the temptation to think is fiercely resisted in most of these groups. There is a strident anti-intellectualism within them that not merely discourages but often prevents any original thinking. The leader is the mediator between us and God, he or she has been given the truth by God, and our only concern is to believe and obey it.

The Search for Heroes

One of the paradoxes of today's society is that we appear to have a deep need for people to respect, admire, and emulate. We have a need for heroes. At the same time we take a perverse delight in knocking our heroes down to size. One moment we admire a politician for their clear thinking, and well-defined objectives. The next we are horrified as some scandal levels them in the dust. A sports personality impresses for his humble nature, and gentle spirit – until we realise that this is only a public face and the private reality is very different. We want the ideal and cannot handle the reality.

Sadly we do the same to religious leaders. All too often we set them on a pedestal, and treat them like demigods when they have done little to merit such attention. A Christian magazine recently printed an article on the twenty leading or most influential Christians of the day. Somehow it all seemed so different from the teaching of Christ: 'He who would be great among you should be your servant.' But the desire is there and the cults appeal to that desire. Their leaders are true heroes, their abilities and achievements truly those of superstars.

We want heroes! We want reassurance that someone knows what is going on in this mad world. We want a father or a mother to lean on. We want revolutionary folk heroes who will tell us what to do until the rapture. We massage the egos of these demagogues and canonise their every opinion. We accept without a whimper their rationalisations of their errors and deviations.[5]

Or how about this description of Douglas Arthur, leader of the London Church of Christ and its satellite congregations, in a magazine to celebrate the first ten years of the church – a magazine, incidentally, edited by himself.

The dynamic growth is a natural extension of a dynamic man of God: Douglas Ray Arthur ... His life is a constant stream of energy, wisdom and concern for others. Whatever fatigue he feels is virtually invisible ... D. A. is really an all-rounder: from sporting endeavours like basketball (Douglas could easily be a professional in England) to more sophisticated games like snooker ... On the intellectual front few can match his quick mind, wit, and way with words. Brilliant at expressing himself ... easy-going, fun-loving and his soft blue eyes never reveal a hint of anxiety. 'Worry – what is that?' Douglas jests. 'Come on, let's flip the frisbee.' Yet when he preaches the Word – Watch out! From those same eyes emanate blazing intensity and uncompromising passion for God . . . Douglas is a man of God.[6]

If it is heroes you want, the new religious movements can provide plenty for you to choose from. As we have seen, one of the most common and clearly identifiable features of the cults is that they are built upon strong, articulate, charismatic leaders without whom the movement would founder.

There is, of course, a deeper and more sinister reason for building up these leaders into demigods. The appeal of the cults rests upon the assumption that the leader or guru is in some sense the recipient of a new revelation or new truth. They are therefore closer to God than anyone else – indeed sometimes they believe themselves to be God. They must therefore be seen to be a cut above everyone else, indeed almost perfect if their appeal is to be accepted. Sometimes a whole myth builds up about the background and calling of the leader, which can be shown to be totally false, but whose purpose is to point out or emphasise their infallibility.

The Search for Love

One of the most common features of abusive groups or cults is their use of what has come to be known as love-bombing. It may take many different forms. It may be a simple hug or embrace whenever one meets a fellow-member. It may involve constantly being told how much one is loved and appreciated by the group. It may be being flattered about anything one does, or congratulated on one's progress.

For many it is immensely attractive. They may have known little love in their homes, they may have felt unable to meet the expectations of their parents or peers, and at last someone appears to love them unconditionally. There is an inherent insecurity in many of us, a desire to be loved and to know that one matters, that makes such an approach particularly attractive. Many cult members and ex-cult members would no doubt echo the words of a former member of an East Coast church: 'I never felt I had a family until I became part of this church. Never before had I felt so loved and cared for in every way. They were the first family I ever had.'[7]

Often leaders will stress that theirs is a church that truly loves, perhaps in a way no other does. Enroth, in his book *Churches that Abuse*, quotes a pastor claiming to his people, 'Do you know of any other church in which people are loving each other with that same kind of unconditional love? I don't.'[8]

As we shall see, that love is all too conditional. It may not seem that way while someone is in the group but let them try to leave and see how unconditional the love really is.

The Search for Identity

One of the commonest cries of today is the cry for identity. Who am I? What am I doing? The world seems so impersonal, so frightening, and so vast that it is becoming increasingly difficult to see where we might fit in. A young person can easily feel themselves to be just another pawn in a giant game of human life. The struggle to pass exams, get a job, keep the job, and provide for dependants has become an all-consuming passion, and often people stop to ask if that is all there is. What if they fail? Do they have any place or identity beyond what they can achieve?

Eileen Barker, a lecturer at the London School of Economics and head of the Government-sponsored INFORM, explains it like this: 'These cults appeal to the young, mainly those of above average education and intelligence, generally from middle class or upper-middle class homes, psychologically well-adjusted. Some are from over-protective homes and need to make a statement ... when they cannot succeed in the real world they seek solace in an alternative family of undemanding religious believers.'[9]

Cults offer at once a clear sense of belonging and identity and a chance to make a statement to one's parents or peers. The group offers that sense of élitism, of being one of the few, of being someone important that up till then may have been lacking.

This is undoubtedly been one of the strongest appeals of the cults. From being just a nobody – or so it has seemed – one has become part of an elect few who will change the course of history, and on whom the world depends.

The Search for Meaning

Closely related to the search for identity is the search for meaning. The cry for meaning has been a common one over the years, but has perhaps been exacerbated by the tensions and uncertainties of the twentieth century. So many discoveries have been made, so much progress, that it makes the quest for meaning all the more acute. 'We have reached the moon, but we have not yet reached each other,' said a former leader of the United Nations, U Thant.

It is a search that is reflected in much of the art and music of the day. I grew up in the 1960s and 1970s, where so much of the music was given over, albeit in a rather self-indulgent way, to this search for meaning. This was well expressed by Pink Floyd on their album, *Dark Side of the Moon*.

> Ticking away the moments that make up a dull day,
> You fritter and waste the hours in an off-hand way.
> Kicking around on a piece of ground in your home town,
> Looking for someone or something to show you the way.

Again the cults appeal to that search for meaning. We have the answer, they claim, we offer you a meaning. You no longer need be bored, lifeless, and directionless.

Of course not everyone who feels this way joins a cult. Most, as Pink Floyd would say, simply 'hang on in quiet desperation'. Perhaps what sets apart those who are drawn in by the cults is that they have less to lose in joining. Being for the most part young, they are less likely to be encumbered with children, mortgages, and endless bills.

The Search for Idealism

Most of us pass through a stage in our lives when we are idealists. We imagine a world as we would like it to be, we think that if only enough people thought like us change would be possible, and we look for a way that will enable us to put these ideals into practice. It is true that most idealists are young, and that the passing of years brings with it a certain world-weariness and cynicism.

Again the cults appeal to this search or need. It is often their first line of approach: 'Would you like to contribute to world peace?' . . . 'We are collecting for church unity' . . . 'We want to bring the world together,' etc. Cult leaders are often brilliantly good at imparting a vision of how things could be; they paint on a broad canvas and invite us to see the future with them. They alone, it seems, have the answers we are desperately seeking.

Perhaps this is particularly true for those who are religious. The Church has always been an easy target for attack. It may be its wealth – often more imagined than real – it may be its confused public utterances, or perhaps its seeming compromise with worldly standards. But unquestionably many are disillusioned with what they see. They want a clearer vision, a stronger lead, a more dynamic image. And the new religion provides just that. The leaders are dynamic, the goals clear, and there is a role for everyone.

Cults make much of the failure of the churches (while at the same time claiming, when it suits them, to be on the same side). They are often pointing the finger at those they accuse of misrepresenting the truth. They claim that only they have the pure, unadulterated truth, only they love truly, only they are fully committed, whereas in reality of course they are flawed like everyone else. But the point is made, and keen religious people are attracted.

No doubt one could point to other common factors in those who embrace the teaching of the cults. But perhaps we should not look too far: it is clear that people of all types and in all situations can be attracted and need to be warned. For when it comes down to it there is often little advance notice, and not much obvious explanation.

The vast majority of those caught up in the cults would never have dreamt of getting involved. Indeed before they joined they would probably have been horrified to be told that they were susceptible. Often they may not have been conscious of actually joining, rather at a particular moment they realised that they were 'in' rather than 'out'. As someone has said, 'Most people never join a cult. They just postpone the decision to leave.' It can be a quite unconscious decision, brought on by a certain inquisitiveness and an unwillingness to upset the members of the group.

But many of the decisions we make in our lives are like that. We fondly imagine that all the great or important decisions are taken after much careful thought and perhaps prayer. We believe that we would never be so foolish as to decide impetuously or rashly on something of such import. But that is often not the case. As Albert Speer, Hitler's Armaments Minister, said of his decision to join the Nazi Party, a decision that irrevocably changed the course of his life:

> Quite often even the most important step in a man's life, his choice of vocation, is taken quite frivolously. He does not bother to find out enough about the basis and the various aspects of that vocation. Once he has chosen it he is inclined to switch off his critical awareness and to fit himself wholly into the predetermined career. My decision to enter Hitler's party was no less frivolous.[10]

It should be noted too that the cults are experts in marketing. They have worked out which strategies work and which ones do not. Their presentation is therefore carefully suited to the individual or group concerned. Albert Speer explains in his book how his own presuppositions about Adolph Hitler had been undermined by the way Hitler spoke at the meeting he attended. Expecting a propagandist rant, he instead found himself confronted by a quiet, clear, and compelling speech that drew him in very skilfully. Here, he reasoned, was no populist demagogue, but a powerful visionary. He thus felt able to lay aside all his doubts on the basis of one evening.

What he only later came to realise was that Hitler had very carefully adapted both his message and presentation to the nature of the audience, which consisted largely of intellectual students. On other occasions he showed an altogether different nature. But for Speer the impression left was so deep and profound that he soon joined the National Socialist Party.

Cults and cults leaders are equally skilful in suiting their message to their audience. In an article in the *Daily Telegraph* magazine, Herman Delorme, a former member of the Solar temple cult in Switzerland, explained how he became involved after a meeting with Luc Jouret, the leader.

> I became involved simply through hearing Dr Jouret speak. He was superb talker, calm, positive, and knowing, well versed in science and medicine. He was an attractive man and I always enjoyed him – he taught me a lot and gave me a positive feeling about myself. He gave people a sense of belonging.[11]

If cults are keen to present a good face, they are equally concerned to avoid bad publicity. As a result they are often positively deceitful in their presentation. It may be simply on the level of not admitting who they are – for fear of the effects of previous bad publicity – but it may extend to the details of their message, what can and cannot be said.

> Today, it is . . . quite common for some cult groups to spend huge sums of money on public relations firms. They pay top dollar to experts to help them make a positive 'image' which will enable them to be more effective in pursuing their hidden agendas. They hire marketing specialists to design their recruitment campaigns. They will use anything that works.[12]

I recently attended a meeting at which a member of the Central London Church of Christ was speaking. At the end of the meeting, at which he had tried to give the impression that we were all basically on the same side, he was asked a simple question about which other churches their organisation worked alongside. For some time he simply refused to answer the question, until finally he was forced to admit they did not work with anyone else. Since he knew such an admission would quickly lose him any credibility, he did his very best to evade it.

In many cases very careful instructions are given about what members should say, and how they are to answer questions. Their recruitment strategy is all-important, and often depends on unpleasant truths being suppressed.

Perhaps therein lies a warning for all involved in the propagation of religious faith in general and Christianity in particular. The lure or attraction of the cults is largely, indeed almost entirely a pragmatic one. They spot a need and then develop a strategy for claiming to meet that need. Of course they have a justification for this. The ends justifies the means. Their goal is the propagation of their understanding of truth. The fact that a little truth bending or manipulation of detail needs to go on along the way is to them incidental alongside the greater good of their mission.

Publicity is based on an appeal to those needs they identify. But it is all pragmatic. If one means of presentation does not work, they will find another; if one truth is unpalatable, then they will keep it back until such time as the member is so fully involved that they cannot easily escape, or will not readily question.

The pragmatic approach to a presentation of truth is ultimately immensely dangerous. If our only criterion for judging both what we believe, and how we present it, is how well it goes down with those we are trying to win, we will almost inevitably find the tail wagging the dog. Our beliefs, our understanding of truth, will be conditioned by the response it receives.

For an extreme example of that we need look no further than some TV evangelists in the US. Their stations need a great deal of money to survive, as do frankly their lifestyles. The inevitable result has been the development of a message that may be popular with a materialistic audience, but is a disastrous misinterpretation of the Christian gospel. The message has become that it is all right to be incredibly rich, and that it is not all right to be poor. Riches are a sign of God's blessing, poverty of His judgment. As Christians we should expect to be rich, healthy, and prosperous.

You cannot escape noticing that the message has been driven by the need, the agenda set by the audience. The preachers need a big audience to support their work. They therefore need a message that will be popular with that audience. What matters is what works.

The same tendency creeps in elsewhere. We want success, if we are religious leaders, we want our programmes to work. So if we are not careful we are likely to develop those programmes that work rather than ones that are faithful to truth. I have been to a number of conferences and read numerous books or pamphlets about different programmes in recent years, all of which have claimed to be the way forward. The interesting thing has been that again and again the justification of these programmes has been not that they give a fair, accurate picture of the truth, but that they work. It is a dangerous road to go down. It is the trick of the politician who wants to be elected and therefore cannot dare tell the whole truth. It is the technique of the salesman who desperately wants to make a sale although he knows his product might not be the best or most appropriate on the market. But unless one is to be regarded as on the same level as these, or as trustworthy, it cannot be the style of the one who wishes to pass on religious truth.

Charles Colson, in his compelling book *Who Speaks for God?*, makes this point when he laments that this seems to be the age of lost opportunity for the Church, precisely because we only think pragmatically.

For the church this ought to be the hour of opportunity. The church alone can provide a moral vision to a wandering people; the church alone can step into the vacuum and demonstrate that there is a sovereign, living God who is the source of Truth.

But the church is in almost as much trouble as the culture, for the church has bought into the same value system: fame, success, materialism, and celebrity ... Preoccupation with these values has also perverted the church's message. The assistant to one renowned media pastor, when asked the key to his man's success, replied without hesitation, 'We give the people what they want.'

This heresy is at the root of the most dangerous message preached today: the what's-in-it-for-me gospel.[13]

How different is the thinking and conviction of the New Testament. St Paul in 2 Corinthians states the Christian alternative: 'We have renounced secret and shameful ways; we do not use deception, nor do we distort the word of God. On the contary, by setting forth the truth plainly we commend ourselves to every man's conscience in the sight of God.'

Paul would not try to trick people into accepting the Christian gospel. Nor would he undermine the truth, as he saw it, of the message because it might be a little unpalatable. Rather his concern was simply to explain, as simply and clearly and honestly as he could, the message, and leave the results to his hearers and to God.

This is why people need to be alerted to the danger of the cults. It is not that people should not be free to choose whatever religion they might prefer. It is simply that they should be able to know what it is they are choosing, and what it is that is being offered.

5

THE DEMAND FOR NEW MEMBERS

How do they recruit?

*'Nobody joins a cult. They just postpone the
decision to leave.'*

Anonymous.

The issue of recruiting is fundamental to an understanding of
the cults as a whole. Indeed the only reasons for a member's
existence within a cult are as recruiter and fundraiser. In fact
the two are really the same. Once a new member is added, a
potential source of money has been found, which means the
making of more money for the leadership. Our aim therefore in
this chapter is to see how recruiting is done.

It is important to recognise that almost all cult members will
have been recruited originally. In other words they may not
have been interested in a particular group until approached by
a member; they may not have even heard of them. It was only
when someone approached them on the street, or in the train,
that their interest was aroused. One man heavily involved in
providing information about the different cults says this: 'Out
of the 20,000 cult calls I have received, I have not met one
person who has joined a cult. They do not join; they are
recruited.'

A similar thing could be said of people joining any group or
organisation. Probably the single most important factor would
be the recommendation or invitation of friends. But what sets
the cults apart is that the invitation is usually given not by a

friend, but by a complete stranger. You have never met the person before, you have never heard of the group, indeed you may not know exactly who they arre even when you join.

Most groups aim to involve a person with them so quickly that no conscious decision is made to join. Rather an individual fails to resist the group's approaches, and is irresistibly drawn in.

My wife and I were given a vivid illustration of this when were recently on holiday. We were approached by a friendly young man with a scratch card. We duly scratched the card and discovered – surprise, surprise – that we were the winners of that day's star prize. To collect this prize all we had to do was report to a local hotel and meet some representative. What was not explained was that this person would try to cajole, persuade, browbeat us into buying a form of timeshare. We had to listen to two hours of sales talk – we had been told it would only be sixty minutes – before being invited to sign away £5,000 on the spot to buy into this scheme, and were made to feel guilty about not accepting. Only when we had been through all that were we able to collect our 'prize'. We had never declared any interest in any timeshare agreement, we had never asked for any information, we had never met any of them before, but we were being expected to part with a large sum of money on the basis of a couple of hours' sales patter. It was, I believe, totally dishonest.

The same sorts of techniques are employed by members recruiting for the cults. There is often a similar 'economy with the truth', a lack of information about what is going on, and an expectation of signing up without a proper chance to make investigations. As a former member of the Moonies put it:

> I had not made the decision to join. I had told noone that I even wanted to ... Since there was so much joy, and since such overwhelming acceptance immediately dashed my fears that I might be rejected because I wasn't smart or capable enough, I said nothing to stop all the celebration. I did nothing to keep them from taking me in.[1]

We will look at these manipulatory techniques in two parts. In this chapter we will consider their use in recruitment, then in the next chapter we will consider how similar techniques are used to keep people in the cults, and increasingly exercise control over them. How then do the cults recruit?

Love-Bombing

As has been said before, love-bombing is one of the most basic of all cult techniques. The aim is to make the person feel that they are a unique individual, greatly loved by the group, and they can find a true home here. This is done in a number of ways. It may be by simple bodily contact – with no necessary sexual overtones – touching, taking the hand, hugging. It may be by constant reiteration of the words 'We love you, you are very special', which an be immensely reassuring especially to those who have known little love or affection in the past. It may be by showering the person with constant attention, always flocking around them and smiling at them.

In an anonymous and unfriendly world, love-bombing is a powerful weapon. People can feel so loved, accepted, and cared for that they never get round to asking more fundamental questions about the group. A member of a group that eventually fell apart over allegations of sexual abuse admitted:

> The people were very loving and accepting – it was like joining a family. The Church side of it was not important, it was like a community that drew me in. I was at a vulnerable age and they made me feel accepted. You feel loved by a lot of people and you quickly get sucked into the circle. It's very insidious.
>
> It all happens quite subtly and almost before you realise it, your life exists in a bubble and you have nothing else – you are dependent on them.[2]

There is of course nothing wrong with seeking to befriend a person, nor with spending time with them. If a person cannot find acceptance within a religious community where can he find it? We all need love and acceptance. What is so disturbing is that the love that is offered, seemingly so freely and openly, is in fact conditional. The group may seem like the most loving, caring, and warm group one has ever met. But it is a conditional love, love with a purpose. They love in order to win over to their group or organisation, and when they become convinced that an individual no longer has anything to offer their group, and is no longer interested, the love immediately stops and may be replaced by anger and abuse, often with devastating effects, as we shall see later.

This love is clearly stressed within the group. Members are told that their love is unique, nobody else loves as deeply, or as selflessly as they do. Of course this is all part of the élitism so inherent in these groups, but it is still immensely attractive. As one member stated: 'I never felt I had a family until I became part of this church. Never before had I felt so loved.'[3]

Before we move on there is an important message here for all churches and religious groups. Most Christian organisations or churches would recognise the force of the Great Commission of Jesus in Matthew 28: 'Therefore go and make disciples of all nations'. To take the gospel to an unbelieving world is the great responsibility of the Church. Equally unless people can see a difference in the Church they will not find the gospel very attractive.

This love is not to be conditional, however, only to be shown to those who might respond to the gospel, or those who belong to our group. It is enjoined upon the Christian to 'love your neighbour', not simply those who might pay a dividend. The fundamental problem with so-called love-bombing is that it is not really love at all. It is a form of emotional bribery.

Yet it is a form of emotional bribery for which many can fall. For example, Christians should be aware that an element of pride can easily creep into the sharing of the gospel. They want their church to be successful, they want it to be full, they want to be able to boast about the success of their programmes. So they will try many different methods to achieve this, and that may include some form of love-bombing: making people feel special, flattering them, enveloping them – not because they love them, but because if they feel loved they are more likely to join.

Christians are called to seek to share Christ with people because they love them. They are not called to love them in order to win them. That is conditional love, if it is love at all. It is emotional bribery. When that is the case the moment a person stops showing any interest in the gospel they will be ignored or rejected. Indeed a good test of the reality of a person's love is whether it remains when we reject their philosophy.

Information Saturation

The second technique is what for want of a better expression I will call information saturation. A potential convert is bombarded by all sorts of pieces of information that he cannot assimilate, but which go to make up a seemingly incontrovertible case for the group.

An example of this is the Moonies' strategy of taking people away for weekends, then overwhelming them with seminars, lectures, and discussions until late at night. The result of this is that the prospective member is carried along on a wave of emotion, but without fully understanding what he is being told. The lectures may be on some political or social theme, often given by important sounding people, and are intended to impress. But so intensive is the programme, so hectic the schedule, that there is never a chance to analyse what one is being told, or decide for oneself whether one wants to embrace it.

The pace of the seminar was hectic. We rose at 7 a.m. on Saturday, had morning exercises, breakfast, and then attended lectures until 2 p.m. After lunch and recreation, we listened to lectures until after midnight, pausing only briefly for dinner at 9 p.m. The same schedule was followed on Sunday. When the lectures ended on Monday at 6 p.m., we were greeted by our 'Spiritual parents', who had come to urge us to join the Unification Church.

My resistance had been worn very low by averaging less than five hours' sleep nightly, many hours of lectures, the spiritual atmosphere of Barrytown, and the warm friendliness and sincerity of everyone. All these factors, plus the logic and clarity of the Divine Principle, had overwhelmed me, and I was hooked.[4]

It is a technique that the London Church of Christ have been known to use. You are invited to one of their Bible studies, or at least to study the Bible with one of their leaders. But the Bible study turns out to be an extremely fast and seemingly convincing tour through certain specific verses. There is never enough time to stop and ask questions. One friend of mine was rebuked for trying to look at the context of the passage in which the verse arose. He was even criticised for taking notes, since the only notes they allowed were the ones they had produced. Independent thought of any kind was discouraged, no space was left for it.

It is perhaps a lesson to the church never to bulldoze or browbeat people into an acceptance of the message. What is required is to present it clearly, and openly, and allow the individual to choose for themselves. Again the church must be very careful on weekends away not to bombard people, or take up all their time. They must have space.

Selective Information

This brings us naturally to another common practice, that of selective information. In other words, in recruitment the group is careful to withhold certain pieces of information that might somehow be counter-productive. It may be on the level of the Moonies, refusing to admit who they are, but it can run much deeper. Truths about the group are deliberately withheld until such time as the person is under their control, when they are least able to complain.

A friend caught up in the Church of Christ explained how it was only after his baptism – for them the moment of his conversion – that he realised what commitment would actually involve.

> Soon after I was baptised, I discovered that many of the Church meetings were compulsory. On one Saturday evening, the church was having a concert, I opted not to go because I was studying for an exam. I was challenged about this by a fellow-student who was a leader, and discovered that not only were the special events mandatory, but so were the retreats, evangelism, morning quiet times, bible discussions, conferences, seminars, sector meetings and, of course, financial contributions. In London, members must pledge the amount they are to give, and are held accountable for it. They are followed up regularly by their disciplers for 'Special Mission Contributions'. I was encouraged to move into a flat with another member.[5]

Few, if any, of these things was he told, apparently, before he officially joined the group. It is a common ploy. Again it is one that churches have to watch out for, the hidden agenda. Is there real honesty about the commitment expected of people? Does the church, like Jesus Christ, at times actively dissuade people from making a profession of faith, because of the cost? 'As they were walking along the road, a man said to [Jesus], "I will follow you wherever you go." Jesus replied, "Foxes have holes and birds of the air have nests, but the Son of Man has nowhere to lay his head"' (Luke 9:57–8).

False Promises

Alongside this selective presentation of facts we find the making of false promises. All sorts of benefits are on offer that only this or that group can bring. It may be peace, success at work, the fulfilment of a potential that we had not realised even existed before, or a promise of perfect health.

Again this is really a case of offering people what they want, and thus manipulating them. We first of all decide what it is that most people want – success, security, good health, personal happiness – then formulate a creed which just so happens to meet that desire. Again it comes back to the problem of pragmatism. We will do what works.

Take for instance the modern obsession with materialism. Posters and adverts scream at us that we need this or that product if we are to be real people. Increasingly therefore we are tempted to live beyond our means, or hanker over things we cannot afford. We are thus wide open to any group or teaching that tells us we can be rich, we can have everything we want. This is one of the horrifying messages to which the modern church has been so susceptible. This is a recognised Christian leader:

> You give $1 for the gospel's sake and $100 belongs to you. You give $10 and you receive $1,000; give $100 and receive $10,000. I know that you can multiply, but I want you to see it in black and white ... Give one airplane and receive one hundred times the value of the airplane. Give one car and the return would furnish you a lifetime of cars. In short Mark 10:30 is a very good deal.[6]

Quite apart from the fact that this is almost too ridiculous to be taken seriously – although incredibly some people do – it is outrageous dishonesty. It is appealing to people's worst instincts with bogus promises. Health and wealth are *not* our rights. Indeed one leader who is infamous for teaching such ridiculous notions has even written an article outlining twenty-five reasons why this teaching may not work after all. Of course these reasons are actually put forward in order to protect those whose promises have been shown to be false. One lady telling of how she had been blamed for her own lack of healing, obviously realised this when she said:

> I've discovered that many people want to see me healed (or pretend to be) because my blindness upsets their theological

applecart. It's hard to believe in their beliefs when a disabled person who thanks God for her disability comes along. It's as if their 'faith' won't stand if I don't go along with their agenda. I believe that they want my healing for their own sake, not mine. It might sound harsh, but I don't think they have a thumbnail of faith.[7]

There is a constant refrain within these groups that there is some utopian paradise around the corner, where all troubles will be dealt with, and we can find the perfection, or fulfilment we long for. We are promised better performance at work, a more fulfilling romantic life, more money, greater peace. Whatever we might want, this or that group will promise to deliver it. And by the time the individual realises that these promises are false, they are usually too involved to get out easily.

For the time being the ideal is just round the corner. L. Ron Hubbard, in advertising the benefits of Dianetics, claimed as much: 'It is true that paths are sometimes rough and that travel can be long and tiring. But wait! There are vistas never dreamed of, there are glories never known, there are glories no past glory ever surpassed. These wait for you but only if you accept my legacy and help bring these things about.'[8]

And yet how easily the Christian Church can sell itself in a similar way. We have already touched on those groups that promise health, wealth, and prosperity. But there are other insidious ways in which false promises can be made. It may be the offer of peace, fulfilment, or a trouble-free life, it may be that the commitment and cost involved are underplayed. But very easily superficial promises can be made about the Christian life that mislead and ultimately end in disillusionment.

Blatant Deception

This brings us naturally on to another characteristic, namely blatant deception. Many of these groups tell straight lies. Indeed the tendency to lie is one of their most notable and disturbing characteristics. Lies are told about which group they belong to, what their work involves, the character of the leadership, the state of their financial affairs, articles in the press, about almost anything.

Of course this lying can be given a nice gloss. A man caught up in the Moonies for some time explained how he was never really given honest answers when he wanted to find out about the group: 'I kept asking questions about the community [Moonies]. Everything I was told about it seemed very nice. Later I learned that they told you what they felt you wanted to hear. They were allowed to tell "heavenly lies" to achieve their objectives.'[9]

In fact language within the cults is often seen as something of a movable feast. Words are used that can mean whatever the groups want them to mean. Stripped of their original meaning, they may be used in a way that defies rational explanation. In his book *A Journey Toward Faith*, John Ephland quotes an ex-Rajneesh follower making the following admission:

> Rajneesh does not hold himself responsible for anything he says, because he 'uses words only to take you beyond words'. He admittedly contradicts himself in his effort to confuse you (your mind) so you get to the point of saying, 'Who cares? Nothing makes sense, so what's the use? I give up. I want enlightenment.' What is really being said here is, 'Don't give me responsibility for my own life. I want to have a daddy again, to be a child all over again with no responsibilities.'[10]

Words are used not to communicate truth, but to obscure and confuse so that you abandon your rational senses and simply receive an experience. Put another way, words have been rendered obsolete. This is, of course, incredibly dangerous. Words are the most basic and accurate means of communication that we have. We can communicate by body language, or picture, or music, to some degree. But they are inevitably flawed and can easily confuse. Interpretations can vary.

Words, on the other hand, are designed to clarify, to explain as precisely as possible. If ever we want to make something clear, we have ultimately to use words, whether written or spoken. That is why the Bible makes clear that God is a God who speaks. He is a God who communicates. When we use words to confuse, or we use words loosely, we are no longer able to communicate in a meaningful sense.

This is precisely what happens within so many of the cults. Words are misused, or used to mean whatever the leader of the group wants. Sometimes common Christian words or terms are used, but given totally different meanings so they have a veneer of respectability, but are really conveying something completely different.

Dr Bernard Ramm, an expert on the cults, has written: 'Such biblical notions as sin, guilt, damnation, justification, regeneration, etc. all come out retranslated into a language that is foreign to the meaning of these concepts in the Scriptures themselves.'[11]

But many churches and Christian groups fall into these same traps. Certain things may be exaggerated to make them appear better than they are. It may be the number of people attending a particular church, or the number of recent converts, or a person's own spiritual progress. Figures and egos are massaged simply to make the appeal stronger. Strange insights are justified on the basis of Bible verses made to mean something quite different from their original meanings.

Proof Texting

This tendency to deceive is a notable feature, not least when it comes to the authority claimed for these beliefs. So closely allied to the last point is the practice common among many of the cults of using proof texts, mostly from the Bible, to support their teaching and organisation. Cults are desperate for some form of recognition, and they feel that if only they can produce a Bible text or two it will validate their teachings. These texts are, however, usually quoted out of context, or given meanings totally different from their original ones.

This technique is so widely practised that it merits a closer look. James Sire, in his book *Proof-Texting and Scripture-Twisting*, details about twenty ways in which cults misuse and abuse the Scriptures.[12]

The first is *inaccurate quotation*. A biblical text is referred to but is either not quoted in the way the text appears in any standard translation or is wrongly attributed. All it needs is to sound genuine. An example of this would be the Maharishi Mahesh Yogi who says, in his *Meditations*, 'Christ said, "Be still and know that I am God."' This text is found only in the Psalms. He goes on to say, 'Be still and know that you are God and when you know that you are God you will begin to live Godhood, and living Godhood there is no reason to suffer.'[13]

First he misplaces the verse itself, then he totally reverses the meaning of the verse by misquoting it. The whole point of the verse is that we are to recognise that God is God and therefore quite different from us. He has managed to make the verse say the total opposite, that we are in some way gods.

A second abuse of the Bible is the *twisted translation*. The biblical text is retranslated, not in accordance with sound scholarship, but simply to fit the preconceived teachings of a cult. A classic example of this is found in the Watchtower version of the Bible used by Jehovah's Witnesses. The Witnesses believe that Christ is not God, but only a man, though a very special one. Consequently they are embarrassed by those Bible passages that appear to speak of Christ as God. So they mistranslate them.

The New International Version of the Bible translates John 1:1 as 'In the beginning was the Word, and the Word was with God, and the Word was God.' The Word here, as becomes clear later in the passage, refers to Christ. The Watchtower Bible, however, adds a crucial letter. 'The Word was a god.' There is no doubt from the structure of the verse in the original Greek that the point that John was making was that this Word, God's Word to His people, was truly God. No serious Bible scholar has ever doubted that this was the message John was trying to convey.

In the Watchtower version the whole sense has been changed.

Christ is now no longer God Himself, but just an exalted human being, in a way that others can be. They do similar tricks with other passages, such as John 8:58, where Jesus's words 'I am' were taken by the Jews as a direct claim to divinity. The Watchtower version reads, 'Before Abraham was, I have been', thus missing the whole point of the exchange.

A third abuse is the *biblical hook*. Here a text of Scripture is quoted primarily to grasp the attention of the reader or listener and then followed by a teaching which is so non-biblical that it would appear far more dubious had it not been preceded by a reference to Scripture. An example of this is the use that Mormon missionaries make of James 1:5, which promises God's wisdom to those who ask Him. They follow this by explaining that when Joseph Smith did this he was given a revelation from which he concluded that God the Father has a body.

There is no concern to look at the passage, or discover what it is saying. It is just that by using the verse in this way they feel able to validate teaching that is totally contrary to the rest of the Bible. James 1:5 has nothing to do with Mormon doctrine, but by a clever trick they persuade people that it corroborates it. But by that token we could justify any belief of any kind simply by saying, 'Oh, I asked God for wisdom, so this idea must be right.'

A fourth abuse is that of *ignoring the immediate context*. To be understood correctly a Bible passage must be seen in its proper context. As has often been said, 'A text without a context is a pretext.' In this practice a text of scripture is quoted but then removed from the surrounding verses, which form the immediate framework for its meaning.

Take the London Church of Christ's use of James 2:24. 'You see that a person is justified by what he does and not by faith alone.' If taken on its own this would seem to be a direct contradiction of the doctrine of justification by faith. When you look at the immediate context, however, the meaning becomes clearer. One needs to ask these questions first: what situation is James addressing? What question is he trying to answer? When you study James 2 you find that it is written not to answer the question, How are we saved? but rather, Given that we are justified by faith, what is saving faith? That is the whole force of verse 14. 'What good is it, my brothers, if a man claims to have faith, but has no deeds? Can such faith save him?' The two key words here are 'claims' – in other words, someone may claim to have faith, but is the claim true? – and 'such' – in other words, is that faith the sort of faith that saves?

What James therefore is trying to establish is not the basis of our salvation – they all agree that a person is saved by faith. He is merely trying to establish what that faith is. Faith is clearly not just having a belief in God. 'You believe that there is one God. Good! Even the demons believe that – and shudder' (2:19). Rather faith is a belief in God that results in a change of life. Where there is no change, James argues, there is no real faith. But you see how one verse, read outside its context, can easily be made to say something it was not intended to.

Another technique sometimes used, totally brazen in its dishonesty, is that of *word play*. Here a word or phrase is used from a biblical translation as though the original revelation had been given in that language. Mary Baker Eddy, founder of Christian Science, says the name Adam consists of two syllables, A and Dam. The word dam means obstruction. Therefore the name of the first man, Adam, indicates the obstruction that exists between man and His Creator. But Adam is merely a transliteration of the Hebrew word meaning man. It has nothing to do with dams or obstructions.

Another error of which Mary Baker Eddy was guilty was that of *the figurative fallacy*. This consists of mistaking literal language for figurative language, or vice versa. Mary Baker Eddy interprets the word 'evening' as 'Mistiness of moral thought', when it simply means evening. The Mormons interpret 'thou shalt be brought down and speak out of the ground' (Is. 29:1–6) to refer literally to God's Word in the Book of Mormon being taken out of the ground, when it is meant figuratively.

This sort of spiritualisation of Bible verses is not, sadly, confined to the cults. All too often Christian writers have taken texts and read the most extraordinary allegorical interpretations into them. This is particularly the case when a group wants to justify a particular religious experience. As an example, it is a little disturbing that one of the justifications used for the Toronto Blessing, in a book written by a leader in the Toronto Airport Church, is Psalm 23: 'He makes me lie down in green pastures.'[14]

Whatever one's views of the Toronto Blessing – and there is much controversy within the Church about it – such a text can surely not be brought in as evidence. The 23rd Psalm has been read, studied, and cherished for three thousand years without anyone ever suggesting that lying down in green pastures has anything to do with a state of religious semi-consciousness. The trouble is that if we allow that sort of interpretation to go unchallenged we have no means of testing anything against the teaching of the Bible. Effectively the Bible comes to mean anything we want it to mean. Verses can be read out of context in whatever way we wish, and used to justify anything. This is highly dangerous. The Bible simply cannot mean whatever we want it to mean.

Another closely-related error is that of *speculative readings of predictive prophecy*. Any student of the Bible knows that there are certain passages that are notoriously difficult to interpet – parts of Ezekiel or Daniel in the Old Testament, or in the New Testament the book of Revelation. These can easily be open to misinterpretation. There is no unanimous agreement among scholars as to what the passages do mean. It is precisely because of this that we should be extremely wary of basing any religious schema upon them. Yet these prophecies often form the basis for cult theology.

To take an example, Ezekiel 37:15–23 speaks of the stick of Judah and the stick of Joseph. This is interpreted in Mormonism to refer to the Bible and the Book of Mormon. Now there is nothing in the text to suggest that. One would only believe that if one started with a certain assumption about the book of Mormon. There is a world of difference between reading something into a text and reading something from it. The Bible never once mentions the Book of Mormon – indeed the Book is quite contrary to the teaching of the Bible – and there is no possible justification for reading such thoughts into these passages.

Many cults do in fact derive their basic teachings from precisely those parts of the Bible that are so difficult to understand. Whenever a Jehovah's Witness comes to the door, they seem unable to resist delving into the more obscure parts of the Book of Revelation. Perhaps this is partly because they know the listener will be ill-equipped to answer, but it is also surely because the passages are sufficiently complicated that nobody will be able to contradict.

Then there is the error of *saying but not citing*. Here the Bible is referred to but not directly quoted. Erik von Daniken, author of the book *Chariots of the Gods*, is guilty of this. He writes, 'Without actually consulting Exodus, I seem to remember that the Ark was often surrounded by flashing sparks . . .'[15] It is perhaps fortunate that he never does consult Exodus because if he did he would find no such passage. The nearest is in Revelation 11:19, where the Ark is in heaven. It is another example of the Bible being used to lend authority to a theory which is directly contrary to its teaching.

Another is *selective citing*. Here a cult will only quote a part of the whole, so as to make it say whatever one wants. Again the Witnesses are guilty of this: they use John 10:30, 'I and the Father are one', to show that Jesus was only claiming unity in 'agreement, purpose, and organisation' with the Father, rather than actually claiming divinity. However it is clear from John 10:33 that the Jews thought Jesus was claiming to be God, and there are many other passages in the New Testament in general and John's Gospel in particular that do point to Jesus as God.

Then there is the danger of the *'obvious' fallacy*. This is where by the use of the words 'obvious' or 'clearly', something is assumed to be the case which is actually far from being either obvious or clear. It is akin to the politician who, wishing to confuse an issue, begins by saying, 'Let's be absolutely clear about this', or 'We have made our position clear on this on many occasions'.

One could go on. There are other ways in which the Bible is treated not as a serious book in its own right, but simply as a repository of proof-texts. These are used to prove whatever an individual group wants it to prove. The Bible is misused, misquoted, misrepresented, and spiritualised.

But, as has been said often before, the churches have been guilty of just the same things. I am not sure whether the church has ever before been so concerned to talk about the 'biblical perspective' and yet so ignorant of the Bible itself.

In his classic book, *Lectures to my Students*, C. H. Spurgeon spends a whole chapter on the danger of misusing the Bible, and particularly spiritualisation – the art of making an allegory out of a plain Bible text. He records the preacher who spoke on the text from Proverbs, 'He that loveth pleasure shall be a poor man: he that loveth wine and oil shall not be rich.'

The meaning of this verse, according to Spurgeon's preacher, was this: 'he that loveth pleasure' was the Christian who enjoys the means of grace. 'Shall be a poor man' means that he will be poor in spirit. 'He that loveth wine and oil' refers to enjoying covenant provisions and the wine and oil of the gospel. 'Shall not be rich' means that he shall not be rich in his own esteem.[16]

Of course that text had nothing to do with the interpretation placed upon it by the preacher. It was just a convenient hook on which to hang some particular thoughts. It is not that the thoughts are necessarily wrong, it is simply that the text did not mean what he made it out to mean. But if we take such liberties with the Bible there is no protection against error. The Bible is not an existentialist handbook, where everything means whatever you want it to mean. For the Christian it is God's Word, entrusted to the church to be faithfully studied and correctly taught (2 Tim. 2:15).

In summary, the recruiting tactics of the cults act as a strong warning. We can admire their enthusiasm, and their zeal, but we must not ape their methods. A true presentation of Christian truth must be faithful to the Bible message, spotless in its integrity and truthfulness, and open in its intentions. It must not come with a hidden agenda, or apply unnecessary pressure. There is no need to distort the message or deceive the hearers. There need be no fear of the seeming simplicity of the message or doubting of its power. It is the gospel that is 'the power of God for salvation' (Romans 1:16), not any human misrepresentations of it.

6

THE DESTRUCTION
OF PERSONALITY

How do they control?

*The man who cannot control himself becomes
absurd when he wants to control others.*

Isaac Arama

We looked in the last chapter at how people are drawn into a group often without fully realising what sort of group it is. But why do they stay in the group when they do realise what it is like?

It has to be admitted that many people within the groups appear happy and fulfilled. If you were to suggest that they belonged to a cult they would laugh at you, or write you off as an unbeliever. They are happy as they are, they know a peace, or joy, or contentment they have never known before; why should they want to leave the group? The people are so friendly, kind, and loving, they see no reason to move. It is therefore very hard to convince someone that the group they belong to is a cult unless they already have some inkling that things are wrong.

One thing that the cults are very clever at is getting a person to make a commitment as soon as possible. They may ask a person to commit themselves financially at the first opportunity. They reason that if they can get someone to make a financial commitment they are more likely to turn up next time.

They may not let you go until they have managed to sign you up for their next meeting or weekend away – and taken your money. All the time subtle pressure is applied that makes it hard to say no without disappointing them or feeling guilty. What they are trying to do is force you to become so committed to the group that you will find it extremely hard to leave.

Once a person begins to grasp the weaknesses of a movement, however, and to ask questions about it, the worm begins to turn. And suddenly all sorts of pressures are applied, emotions are tugged, and tactics employed. It is at this stage that one sees the conditionality of their love, and blinkeredness of their vision.

But once involved in a group, how do they operate? How do they ensure that a person stays a faithful and committed member?

Group Pressure

The first and most obvious technique applied is that of group pressure. In all groups there is a careful and systematic attempt to build up a group identity and character that makes it very difficult for anyone to stand against it. Something is right because the group says it or believes it.

This can be done at many different levels but we need to be aware how vulnerable we all are to this type of group pressure. A telling illustration of this is provided by the studies conducted by Stanley Milgram in 1963 and 1974. Ordinary people were invited in off the streets, and offered $4 for an hour's experiment. They were each asked to play the role of a teacher. They sat on one side of a transparent screen, while on the other sat the object of the experiment, the learner, who was strapped in to a harness which could give him electric shocks. The teacher was then requested to ask various questions of the learner.

Every time the learner got the answer to a question wrong the teacher was expected to administer an electric shock to him. All the while the teacher could see the learner and watch his reaction. As the learner made more mistakes so the shock was made progressively greater, from 'slight shock' to 'danger: severe shock'.

As the experiment went on, and as the learner received ever

more severe shocks, he could be clearly seen, by the teacher, shouting and cursing. He started to kick the wall at 300 volts. Often the teacher would plead with the experimenter to halt, but he insisted: 'Please continue', 'The experiment requires that you continue', etc.

Milgram found that 65 per cent of the teachers went all the way to the limit of 450 volts, and not one stopped prior to the learner kicking the wall.

Of course, the experiment was a hoax; the learner was an actor, and he received no electric shock at all. But the striking thing was that the teacher did not realise this, and was prepared to administer very heavy shocks, even to the point where it was supposed to be life-threatening.

Milgram was able to deduce from this that we find it very hard to go against the crowd, or against what is expected of us, even when it involves causing great pain to someone with whom we have no quarrel. In the experiment ordinary judgment was suspended, as though normal rules of human behaviour no longer applied. It is precisely this human characteristic that the cults are liable to exploit, except that they put people under a great deal more pressure than in the experiment.

So what is the aim of this group pressure? Primarily its aim is to produce conformity to a norm so that all criticism and dissent are ruled out. This is in fact a good litmus test. What effect does the group produce in its members? If the overall effect is one where the individual's character is subsumed into that of the group, where individuality is discouraged, even squashed, then we are on dangerous ground.

This is one of the signs that family members or parents are apt to notice first of all. Perhaps when they hear that their son or daughter has joined a religious group they may be uncertain, but willing to see how things develop. It is only when they see the individual lose their sense of humour, and their personality, that real fear sets in. Very often I have found anxious parents or friends pointing to this stunting of personality as their greatest worry. Flavil Yeakley, in his book *The Discipling Dilemma*, makes exactly this point:

> They tend to make people over after the image of a group leader, the group norm, or what the group regards as the ideal personality ... They are made to feel guilty for being what they are and inferior for not being what the group wants them to be.[1]

In analysing the Boston Church of Christ, Yeakley highlights the same tendency. The Church was, he claims,

> producing in its members the very same pattern of unhealthy personality change that is observed in studies of well-known manipulative sects. The data ... prove that there is a group dynamic operating in that congregation that influences members to change their personalities to conform to the group norm ... The Holy Spirit changes people when they become Christians, but not by making us identical in psychological type. The growth that comes from the Holy Spirit produces a body with many different members that perform many different functions in many different ways.[2]

True authority, as Yeakley rightly points out, should never have the effect of restricting someone's personality. Authority, rightly exercised, should always enhance a person's personality, bring it out, enable it to blossom, rather than destroy it. John Stott, in his book *I Believe in Preaching*, suggests that this is the distinction between true and false authority:

> Christians distinguish between true and false authority, that is, between the tyranny which crushes our humanity and the rational, benevolent authority under which we find our authentic human freedom.[3]

Group pressure, then, is used to conform people to a particular mould. But it is also used to enforce discipline, and bring so-called recalcitrants back into line. I vividly recall a leader in the London Church of Christ speak of how he and six other leaders had one evening taken an hour to 'persuade' an individual that he was out of order and bring him back under their control. It seemed that it would have been almost impossible for anyone to resist that sort of pressure. Ronald Enroth speaks of just that sort of pressure:

> You have one person on one side of the table, with an array of men on the other side. A domineering person is telling you you're wrong, why you're wrong, that you need to repent, and then, one by one, all the rest of them agree wholeheartedly. The targetted person has a tremendous psychological onslaught to deal with. More often than not he ends in tears and repents, and is either eventually restored to favour or leaves the fellowship.[4]

You would have to be either a very strong character and sure of your ground, or very stubborn, to resist.

Again, this is a lesson the churches should heed. Sometimes in churches or groups there are strong pressures to conform, to go with the crowd, which cause people to make decisions based not on clear thinking or conviction, but an innate desire to please and fit in. Over the years church youth work has been plagued by false decisions of commitment in this way. Great care must be taken to ensure that any appeal for Christ is rooted not in emotion or peer pressure, but in the force and power of the message itself.

Systematic Manipulation

A second technique of the cults is what I would call systematic manipulation. A member is clearly targetted and pressurised to take a certain course of action. It may be by sleep or food deprivation. There is little doubt that certain groups very deliberately seek to wear down a person's self-defence by these methods. Weekend conferences where sessions last long into the night, church houses where the individual is expected to be up late at night and early in the morning, and small food rations are all used to strip a person of their ability to withstand pressure. At certain conferences watches are handed in at the outset so that people are encouraged to lose all concept of time.

Then when the defences are down, they begin to pressure you into making the decision they want. Ronald Enroth describes the experience of someone involved with The Way International of Paul Wierwille.

> When you are at this point is when they really get heavy and start coming down on you, reading Scriptures to you, explaining to you what they mean. You are at the point where you are so physically and mentally fatigued that you take exactly what they say for granted. You get to the point where you are so involved ... you are so brainwashed, that anything they tell you, you are going to believe. It took The Way ministry about one month to accomplish this.[5]

Another common way in which a person is similarly abused is the giving or withholding of praise. We all want to please by nature, and particularly in a group setting we fear falling out of favour. This is therefore often used against someone. In the London Church of Christ people are both praised and criticised publicly. On one occasion a member was publicly rebuked for daring to attend another church. It is hard to overestimate the power of this sort of public criticism. Having been accepted and praised in the past suddenly there comes an awareness that you are out of favour, that somehow you have slipped up. You may not even be aware of what you have done, only that you are in some way at fault. You then have to win your way back into favour, and are prepared to do almost anything to achieve that.

It is a technique that seems to have been used in the Nine O'Clock Service in Sheffield. A member of the service spoke about the hold the leader had over them, and how this power was exercised:

> X was very clever. He very quickly would suss out a person's vulnerability and use it to isolate and manipulate them mercilessly. He would ensure people's lives were changed ...

People would be encouraged to feel that they belonged and then they would be rejected. They would have to struggle hard to get back in. It was not blatant. He was far too clever for that. It was subtle, like water from a tap, dripping on a stone. You would feel you were being punished for something, but you would not know what you had done wrong. Lives were being manipulated.[6]

If what drew a person to the group in the first place was the love that was shown, if what was found most attractive was the acceptance, how devastating to find that love withdrawn. It is a callous way of exercising control.

Notice too how it stems criticism. All those who are seen as a threat are themselves attacked, for their rebelliousness, or their lack of loyalty. All criticism is turned back upon itself. If you dare to suggest that the group might be wrong in any way, you are told that the real fault lies within you:

Whenever I questioned these things, the following responses were most commonly given. 'That's not the issue – the issue is you're not broken.' 'It's in the Bible.' 'I'm disappointed in you, how could you be questioning now?' or 'Brother, you just need to change.'[7]

The aim is to break a person's will. A weak-willed person will never stand against the authority figure, but will dutifully do what they are told. A strong-willed one is a threat, and is attacked openly, and their commitment questioned:

I was seen as a threat. I was a strong person. He would attack people by placing doubt on their commitment and loyalty to the NOS. He would question time spent with friends and family outside.[8]

Competition

Another way in which members are kept under control is the use of competitiveness, or the building up of a competitive spirit. Members are encouraged to outdo one another in their commitment. In some ways this is a little like two men vying to win the affections of a woman. Each does his best to outdo the other in the sacrifices he is prepared to make, and the lengths to which he is prepared to go. Both are desperate for that sign that they are the favoured one.

Such competitiveness is very valuable for the leader. If everyone is kept on their toes, desperate to win the seal of approval, then the leader can control. It is something the Moonies have not been slow to utilise:

> Moon also liked to stimulate the highest degree of competition between leaders in order to maximise productivity. He would single out someone who was very successful at recruiting or fundraising (he did this with me), and present that person as a model of excellence, shaming the others into being more successful.[9]

Monitoring

Then there is the constant monitoring of a member's life and behaviour. We have already touched on the discipling and shepherding that is often used by the leadership. In many of the cults there is a very strict system of shepherding which ensures that an individual is monitored for any signs of rebelliousness or disloyalty.

This is of course given a pious justification. In some groups obedience to the leader is seen as obedience to God – in some cases because the leader is actually seen as God, in others because he is at the very least a mediator between others and God. So when a person stands against the group or leader, it is seen as an act against God Himself.

For this reason, people's lives are meant to be an open book to their leadership. They must reveal all their deepest secrets and weaknesses. Further they are required to inform on others when they are in danger of falling:

It is a worldly concept, inspired by the devil, which makes us think it is doing someone a favour to keep their sins hidden from those who are in a position to help. Remember we are our brother's keeper. Please do your friends a favour when you see them making serious mistakes; tell your pastor or an elder so something can be done in time.[10]

Notice the clever way in which the informing is dressed up. People must inform on their brothers and sisters because that way the leaders can 'help' them. In reality it is not help they want to offer, but control. As Yeakley goes on:

The discipling hierarchy thus becomes a glorified informant network. As such, it is an effective means of control ... Those being discipled were told what courses to take in school, what field to major in, what career to enter, whom to date or not to date, and even whom to marry and not to marry.[11]

The Boston Church of Christ and its satellite churches and congregations have gained an infamous reputation for this sort of manipulation. And in some ways what makes it so deceptive is the fact that behind the practice lies a good principle. Many Christian traditions have the practice of the 'spiritual director', someone who acts as a sounding-board cum adviser cum confidant. It is a voluntary arrangement whereby one sees one's spiritual director maybe once every couple of months and is able to talk through any issues. Many find it an enormous help. But note it is a voluntary arrangement, and it is confidential.

So when Kip McKean, in a talk entitled 'Why do you Resist the Spirit?' given in 1987, says, 'No one can do it on their own. Everybody needs ongoing discipleship. You are a disciple of God until you die and you are a disciple of someone else until you die,' in some ways one can agree. But it is the nature of the discipleship, and the control thereby exercised that is so danger-ous. The relationship is not one of mutual trust, where advice is given in confidence. It is one where obedience, unquestioning obedience is expected. Jerry Jones, in his book *What does the Boston Church Teach?*, makes this point:

> A disciple is one who obeys his discipler even if he doesn't comprehend what he's told. Because he wants to have a teachable heart, he will fully obey and be totally obedient even if what he's asked to do is contrary to what he would normally do or think. To distrust the person God had put in his life is equal to distrusting God and his faith in God is shown by his faith in his discipler.[12]

So while the principle of the spiritual director, or elder brother, is a good and right one, here it has been perverted to become something quite different. It has become a means of control, monitoring and manipulation. As Jones goes on to say:

> Everyone's Christian life was under scrutiny by someone, assigned by some level of authority; each member was confronted with observed faults, issued counsel, and followed up; each was encouraged to know the true state of his own soul, its sins and weaknesses, and to confess those openly and honestly to others who have ministry and authority over him.[13]

Spiritual Blackmail

From this it is a short step to some form of spiritual blackmail. Information gained through the discipling relationship is used against the individual. This apparently was the case in the Nine O'Clock Service in Sheffield. Widespread abuse by the leadership was going on but members who stood against it risked being exposed themselves. One former member spoke of how she had apparently been victimised in this way:

> After rejecting advances of one leader she was brought before the leader himself. After rejecting his advances, he allegedly took revenge with savage public putdowns, revealing intimate

knowledge of her background ... he accused her of being defensive and having a problem with authority. Friends refused to take her calls, or told her they could not see her because she was destructive.[14]

In other churches the same sort of technique is adopted. In the Sunday bulletin of one church in California could be found the following announcement:

Mrs X refuses to stop the soul-damning sin of gluttony. She uses every excuse to stay fat. She also has a bitter, complaining attitude towards this church. The Board of Elders recommends that she be transferred to [another church] until she is willing to stop her sin of gluttony. The members of this church will vote on dropping and barring Mrs X next Sunday ... if Mrs X wishes to repent, she needs to see [the leadership] and express a willingness to stop complaining and lose weight.[15]

There is another form of spiritual blackmail that may be employed. Because the group has claimed to be the only true church or religion, however much one may wish to leave the group one is fearful of turning one's back upon God. However flawed it may have become, this group is the true faith, and to leave it would be to leave God. This is something that is played on mercilessly by group leaders. It may even be that a number of group members feel the same way, but nobody wants to be the first to blow the whistle. A member of the Boston Church of Christ admitted as much:

... nobody wants to confess that they're the only one in the group that doesn't have any clothes on, so they just kind of jump on the bandwagon. They get into it even if it doesn't seem right to them because they don't want to miss out on what God has for them. They don't want to be left out of 'the bride', left out of 'the rapture', not be part of the 'man-child ministry'.[16]

This leads us to the whole subject of leaving a cult. In some ways this is the most difficult time of all. While a person is with the group, and going along with everything that is said and done, there are really no problems. That is why telling someone that they are involved in a cult is often pointless. An outsider may see the difference it has made, and the damage being done to the individual, but the chances are that the member will not. They have no difficulties, and are not in any way aware of the pressures, while they go along with them. But when the questions rise, and the doubts come in, then the problems mount.

Any criticism of the group, or questioning of its methods, will inevitably evoke a critical response. You will be told that it is you who is to blame, and that it is you who needs to change. If only you were more committed, more obedient, then all would be clear: 'I was not happy in the church. My discipler would constantly re-assure me that if I would evangelise more it would all become more clear to me.'[17] In other words, the fault will never lie with the group but with the individual. All sorts of pressures may be brought to bear upon you – emotional, spiritual, personal. As one man who became caught up in the Moonies expressed it:

> I stayed with them for about a week. It was a very exciting week and at no stage did I really feel that I was being kept against my will. After a week I decided, OK, this was great, everything was fantastic but I'd like to move on. Janice [the counsellor] said 'Oh, you can't move on, you can't move on, we have a weekend retreat coming up at our retreat place, Camp K. It's only $20 to go for a weekend . . . surely you can wait another few days and go to Camp K and hear Dr Moses Durst, he is one of our best brothers and one of our best lecturers'. For the first time I had a feeling that I was being trapped, mentally imprisoned in the community.[18]

I have often found that it is at this stage that the person is prepared to listen to critical comments about the group. They have begun to realise that all is not well, but they are not sure what and why. They feel a deep unease, but they cannot quite put a finger on it. At the same time this is when the group will exert the greatest and most painful pressure:

> The amount of mental pressure that was put on me to stay was really unbelievable. All the friends I had made in the last few weeks came up to me and started crying . . . I really felt terrible. I said 'Look, I'm leaving and that's it.' I was very frustrated, very mixed up and really didn't know what to do.[19]

For this reason it is vital that those who deal with members and ex-members know as much as possible about the group. They will need to be able to show them that the group was definitely wrong and that it was not their weakness that led to them leaving. Ronald Enroth comments,

> It is an extremely important factor whether a person leaves an abusive-church situation knowing that the group was wrong, or believing that he was wrong and is now sinning against God.[20]

I have frequently met ex-members of a group who are still haunted by feelings of emptiness and guilt. I can think of one girl who left her group because she was unwilling to abide by the moral teaching she had received, but was still convinced that this church alone was right.

The cost of leaving can be very high. It can be emotionally devastating, not simply because one has left a group of close friends – and once one is involved in a cult one tends to lose any outside friends – but also because those who were once friends are now enemies and will have nothing to do with you. Someone who leaves a cult is an outcast, cut off from the truth and from God for ever:

> We who left were labelled 'rebels against God' and cut off from fellowship with those who remained, those we had

worshipped, worked and prayed with as a close-knit family for five years. It was like a divorce.[21]

How insidious and frightening such remarks are. Leaving that church is equated with leaving God. The pastor sees himself as taking the place of God so that not to follow him is not to follow God. Is it any wonder that so many find it incredibly hard to leave? But leaving is not only hard spiritually, it is also hard emotionally. It feels genuinely like a bereavement. The group has become one's family, and now one is separated from it for ever. There is no chance of remaining friends, because one is perceived as betraying those who were one's friends.[22]

Members of the group are liable to write or ring up and be violently abusive. They will assure you that you are going to hell, they will curse you, and do all they can to make you come back. A former Jehovah's Witness received a letter with these words: 'You are the whore of Babylon! You are the devil incarnate – back to the pit you stinking vomit. Keep away from us, don't come near us – you will be destroyed just as the Tower of Babel.'[23]

It is hard to overemphasise the impact that such treatment can have upon a person. Remember that many will not have had to make an independent decision for years. Everything has been decided for them by the group. Suddenly they are thrown out into the world, having lost their security, their friends, and their family. The chances are that they will have lost all their previous friendships and family ties during their time with the group. They may feel too ashamed to eat humble pie. They are still uncertain as to whether they have done the right thing, and feel obsessively guilty.

For this reason there are many agencies to help individuals come to terms with life again, with making decisions, finding a job, and a new security. It can take a long time for them to rebuild trust in other people. They may well regard any religion with the same sort of fear and loathing with which they now regard their former group.

Again, before we move on, there are lessons that the Church

needs to learn. As I said earlier, within much of the Church there is an obsession with numbers and success. This may be for financial reasons – the Church after all does need to pay its way. But it may also be to do with power and the egotism of a particular leader. It becomes very easy for a leader or a church to act in a way not at all unlike the behaviour within the cults.

Group pressure is very powerful, and one must be extremely cautious about using peer pressure to force decisions out of people, particularly young people. How selective and conditional is love? How far is information used about members of churches as a means of controlling them? How do leaders react to criticism? Is it turned around on the one criticising? Is a competitive spirit deliberately instilled so that members are eager to please the leadership and win their favour?

And what of the effect upon the members of churches? Is the result of teaching and practice that people begin to lose their individuality and become clones of the leadership – aping them in their habits, mannerisms, and speaking? Do people increasingly look to the leadership to make all sorts of decisions for them, or is the leadership of such a nature as to allow people to decide for themselves? What is the attitude to those who wish to leave the church? Will no other church ever be good enough for them? I am aware of one church – well known in evangelical circles – where a member was told not to move to another town because there was no church belonging to that organisation in that town. No other church, apparently, would do.

As the old saying goes, 'People who live in glass houses should not throw stones.' If Christians are to point the finger at the cults or new religious movements they must be careful to ensure their own house is in order.

7

THE DEMISE OF ERROR

Where does it end?

'I am a thinker, I am your brain. When you join the effort with me you can do everything in utter obedience to me.'[1]

Sun Myung Moon

We have so far looked at the different features of cults, and seen how easily and quickly they can beguile the unwary. We have been struck by the enormous number of cults that have sprung up, and continue to do so in the Western world. But several questions then arise. What happens to them? Do they blow themselves out? Do they in time become more mainstream and acceptable? Or does something more cataclysmic result?

In some ways all three are true. There are many groups that simply fade into oblivion, perhaps because members realise that the claims are too preposterous or because they are shown to be false. Some years ago von Daniken's theory about Christ being a spaceman was all the rage. Once his books were subjected to anything like proper critical scrutiny, however, it became obvious that the theory simply could not stand up.

Other groups and other theories have met with a similar fate, although it is surprising how long an idea can survive after the basis upon which it has been built has been eroded. For a number of years it has been known that the Guru Maharaj Ji was a fraud, but he still has his devotees who probably think of him as misrepresented and unfairly maligned. Again, to outside observers it is apparent that Rev. Moon is a convicted fraudster, but to his followers he is still the Messiah. We cannot place too much reliance, it appears, on people's willingness to confront reality when involved in one of these groups.

But in most cases where there is an obvious deceit or lie at the centre of one of these groups it becomes apparent in time. This is obviously true of those groups who expect some apocalyptic nightmare to take place at a particular time. Such a fate tends to await those groups that insist, against all the teaching of the New Testament, on putting a date to the end of the world.

A second possible scenario is that a group becomes more accepted in the mainstream of religious life. I have referred a number of times to the Mormons as a cult. I do in fact believe that they exhibit a number of the features of the cults, not least that they have grossly distorted and misrepresented the teaching of the Bible. Any group that can add to the Bible in the shameless way that they have can have little cause for complaint when it is pointed out to them.

Mormons and Mormonism have, however, been accepted into the mainstream of public life, particularly in the US. The State of Utah is largely given over to the Mormons and they have formulated a system that goes beyond merely religious boundaries. Mormonism has become more than a religious belief, it has become a whole community identity whereby believing certain tenets of faith is less important than being a member of a particular community. In saying that one is not seeking to defend their beliefs, it is simply to state the obvious that Mormonism has become so bound up in a culture and community that proving their beliefs are wrong will not change that identity. Indeed many of the Mormon leaders are aware of the false claims of Joseph Smith and Brigham Young, and that their version of history does not stand up to critical scrutiny, but have not found it convenient to admit it. Too much stands to be lost.

It is with those other cases, where the group neither fades immediately away nor becomes part of the mainstream, that I am particularly concerned in this chapter. History is full of examples of religious groups that have gone badly astray and ended up in some disaster. We know only too well from the last twenty-five years what appalling disasters can result from a group that believes it has the unique truth and will not listen to anyone else.

History, both ancient and modern, suggests that there are three directions in which abusive power tends to lead a group. Not every cult or abusive group will inevitably lead there, but there is a very strong chance that it will. Perhaps it is here that a study of Church history is so fascinating and revealing. All modern heresy is really a reworking of previous heresy, and what we see today within these groups is no more than has been seen in the Church throughout the two thousand years of its history.

Take Gnosticism. This was, as mentioned earlier, the teaching that while Christianity was fine, a person needed an extra knowledge, γνωσις, for true salvation. The earliest proponent of this teaching is reckoned to have been Simon Magus in Acts 8, but it found its fullest development in the teachings of Valentinus and Basilides. They taught some quite bizarre views about the material world and about celestial beings. People had to be initiated into these heavenly mysteries.

But what is important about them is where these teachings led. In some instances, because they believed that salvation was not dependent on behaviour but on the knowledge of an innate pneumatic nature, they descended into an extreme libertinism, or gross immorality. They believed that they could not be sullied by any external 'mud', so how they behaved with their bodies was a matter of complete indifference.

One could also point to the perfectionist movement of the late nineteenth century. This claimed that it was possible to attain a state of moral perfection in this life. Unfortunately it ended in one of two ways. Either it resulted in a state of disillusionment, as people recognised that it was simply not possible, at least for them, or interestingly it ended in moral disarray, with stories of sexual misconduct.

The reason is not hard to find. Someone claims to have

reached a state of sinless perfection. They find that they are confronted with sexual temptation. Either therefore they were wrong before and are not perfect after all, or they were right, in which case, since they are perfect, these desires cannot be wrong. If these desires are not wrong, it cannot be wrong to yield to them. It may seem perverse, but there is a strange logic to it, and as we shall see, there is much attempt to justify moral misbehaviour on the grounds that it is not really wrong at all.

What then are these three directions?

Sexual Scandal

The first result is, as I have suggested, sexual scandal. I am not claiming that all groups end this way, but sadly many do. The sexual urge is very deep in all of us. We often have to face and overcome sexual urges and temptations and perhaps that has never been more so than in today's sex-obsessed society. When you mix a society where there is such emphasis on sexual expression with groups where certain leaders are already set above the law, as it were, you have an extremely potent cocktail. If you look at the number of groups which have gone down this road it is alarming.

We mentioned in an earlier chapter the accusations against the Rev. Moon. We are aware of the horrifying accusations against David Berg and the Family, where child abuse seems to have been common. Indeed Berg developed an ingenious way of justifying such abuse: 'If what we do is in love, against such thing there is no law. All things are lawful unto me and to the pure all things are pure.'[2]

We have seen the same in the Divine Light Mission, with Guru Maharaj Ji, with David Koresh of the Branch Davidians, and most recently with the Nine O'Clock Service in Sheffield. Too often when leaders manage to create a situation where they are above criticism they appear to use it for their own sexual gratification.

So we need to notice three things about this. First there is often a 'theology of sex' that is developed. It has long been said that the Church has been involved in sexual repression over the centuries. The Church has taught, supposedly, that sex is 'dirty', only permissible for the procreation of children. It is definitely not something to be rejoiced in, or enjoyed.

Now there may be some truth in this accusation. Perhaps the Church has not been willing enough to admit that sex is a wonderful gift of God, albeit when in its proper context. But even at this stage we need to recognise the slant of the argument. The Church, or rather the Bible, has not taught repression, as is claimed, but self-control (Gal. 5:23, et al.) But in today's society any form of self-control can be represented as 'repression', and 'not being honest about ourselves'.

But see where the argument goes from here. Sex is good, it is argued, and to be celebrated. God made it, we should enjoy it. Therefore when anyone suggests that certain behaviour is overly sexual and not helpful or unbecoming for Christians, they are told that they are repressed and uneasy with their sexuality. What was a Christian virtue – self-control and modesty – has become a sin. To dress sexually is therefore no longer sinful, but an honest way of celebrating a God-given gift. A former member of the Nine O'Clock Service described the thinking in this way.

The message was to be sexual with God. God made us to be sexual and sensual, and we were told to go with that. Sexuality was expressed through dance and scantily-clad women. It seemed OK to be sexy, not just within marriage.

A lot of the women were expressing themselves through their clothing, by wearing short shorts, micro skirts and tight fitting tops. It was a lot of the leaders – the women at the top – who dressed like that. You only seemed to become part of the leadership if you looked glamorous, had a great figure and wore very little.

There were a lot of attractive people there, and [the leader] always seemed to be surrounded by glamorous women. I had a gut feeling all this was wrong. The sexuality was freaking me out. The whole thing was a big sexual fantasy.[3]

Do you see how skilfully Christian thinking has been changed and distorted? Instead of behaving and dressing modestly, members were being encouraged to do the opposite. It was all cloaked in a veneer of spiritual talk. In fact, as the same member explained; 'We were just the little people making his fantasy possible. It was all for his self-gratification.'[4]

Second, we need to recognise the close connection between sex and experience. It has often been remarked that the sexual experience and the spiritual one are closely linked – though I remain to be convinced. But there is no doubt that in certain people's thinking the two are linked. What makes it all the more difficult is that when experience begins to determine what people believe, rather than the other way round, then there is little defence against this sort of theology creeping in.

A church in the United States developed an extraordinary concept of spiritual connections.

The teaching ... encouraged members to have a 'connection' or dance partner ... partners were instructed to stare into one another's eyes, eventually known as 'connecting'. Partners were told they would see Jesus in one another's eyes, and that they were to love their spiritual connection in order to express their love of Jesus ... members were encouraged to spend time with their spiritual connections in a kind of quasi-dating relationship ... physical intimacy often accompanied these 'spiritual' connections. 'Connection love' was supposedly more intense, and even more desirable, than marital love.

There were numerous accounts of adulterous relationships, sexual assault, harshly shunned and rejected dissidents, child abuse, suicides and attempted suicides, broken marriages, child-custody battles, and lawsuits.

The members were told that intimate spiritual experiences with members of the opposite sex, other than one's spouse, could help defeat the demons of jealousy and open up the person to a deepened experience of the love of Christ.[5]

It seems hard to believe that anybody could fall for that sort of insanity. But the reason they did was that they had already abdicated the obligation to use their minds, and had given themselves over to the slavery of an experience-based theology. As one of the members graphically put it:

> We put a premium on spiritual experience. It's shocking to me to see what transpired. Once you're out in the realm of experience, you can't talk Scripture anymore because there's no Scripture that's releveant to something as wild and bizarre as this . . . Everyone was ready to go for anything that seemed spiritual.[6]

The third thing to notice is peer pressure. In a group where so much devotion and respect is accorded to the leadership it becomes incredibly hard to stand against the prevailing views. If everyone else thinks it is OK, how can they all be wrong? Especially when we already believe that this group is really the only correct one. Indeed we begin to think that the real problem must lie within ourselves rather than the group. As another member of the NOS put it:

> We were told we all needed healing and to explore our sexuality. It meant you opened up and were often at your most vulnerable, talking about painful things. You were often in tears.
> You look up to them. You never think they are going to abuse you. I thought maybe that I was responsible for encouraging it . . . the end result was that I felt I was out of order, like I was in trouble for complaining.[7]

This is often the case with instances of child abuse. A child will be aware that things are not right but cannot reconcile that with the natural love and respect he or she feels for the adult. Thus there is enormous confusion, with the child often ending up believing that the fault is really with them. And the comparison is quite apt since in many respects the way the member has given over responsibility for their life to the leader has effectively brought them back into a form of childhood anyway.

Let me say again that not every group ends up in sexual scandal. Indeed many of these groups claim to possess a very strict code of morality. But I am saying that given the conditions in which cults exist, and the uncritical and unquestioning respect in which the leadership is held, there is a very strong possibility that that respect will be abused, often in sexual matters.

Financial Scandal

The second consequence of cult abuse is financial scandal. If the temptation of sexual misdemeanour is very powerful within the groups, the temptation to misuse money is equally strong. Most groups will raise great sums of money through their membership. As we have already said, an enormous commitment is expected of group members, and this is particularly so with regard to money. People often give over their life savings to a group as a sign of their commitment. One member of the London Church of Christ gave his entire year's student grant to the church at the beginning of the year and lived off others for the whole time. He was publicly praised for his commitment, although all it meant was that others had to bail him out.

The same has been said of the NOS: 'A friend gave an inheritance of £5,000. We were encouraged to give as much as we could. I had a run-in with my pastoral leader who wanted me to give more.' 'Everyone gave, whether they were on the dole or not. People were donating their houses and legacies. Companies were giving money too.'[8]

Of course, sacrifical giving is both biblical and admirable. The Bible frequently encourages Christians to give generously. Indeed giving is seen in a number of places as a pre-condition of blessing. But there is all the difference in the world between the generous giving of a congregation, and the greedy acquisitiveness of the leadership in many of these groups. The leadership all too often plays upon the sensibilites of group members to give money, without their being aware of where that money goes.

The Moonies may collect money for 'world mission' or for 'unity among churches', but it does not go towards those ends. It simply goes to line the pockets of the Rev. Moon and his leaders. Followers of the Bhagwan Shree Rajneesh may have given sacrificially, but the only real beneficiary was the Bhagwan himself. Where these practices exist, sooner or later the result is financial scandal: the Rev. Moon was jailed for tax fraud, others are shown up as greedy opportunists.

I was speaking with a member of the Church of Scientology recently who claimed that when L. Ron Hubbard died he left about $840 million. It had caused him to ask very serious questions, not least because the Church was paying him a pittance to work for them.

This affects more mainline groups as well. Probably the saddest feature of the scandals of the tele-evangelists in the US over the last few years has been the appalling cynicism of their fundraising, and the grotesquely affluent lifestyles this has funded. But it should not surprise us. Their teaching has claimed that riches are a sign of God's blessing, but that to gain riches you have first to give. 'Give and it will be given you.' This has the double advantage of holding out to people promises of material wealth – which appeals to their natural desires – while at the same time ensuring that there is a regular supply of money coming in.

Many see the whole cult movement as simply a way of making money. But such was ever the case. The Apostle Paul had to face accusations of seeking financial gain himself as he sought to share the gospel. It seems that religious teachers at the time expected to be paid for their services, so that religious teaching was seen as a lucrative profession. But Paul never wanted anyone to think that he preached the gospel for reasons of financial remuneration: 'Surely you remember, brothers, our toil and hardship; we worked night and day in order not to be a burden to anyone while we preached the gospel of God to you.' (1 Thess. 2:9).

Indeed this refusal to take money was even used as a criticism of his whole ministry. If he did not receive money for his work he surely could not be a true religious teacher. 'Was it a sin for me to lower myself in order to elevate you by preaching the gospel of God to you free of charge? . . . And when I was with you and needed something, I was not a burden to anyone, for the brothers who came from Macedonia supplied what I needed' (2 Cor. 11:7, 9).

Misuse of money is a common temptation among these groups. And in the end it results in serious financial scandal. It may be the appallingly affluent lifestyles of the leadership, compared to the poverty of the members. It may be unpaid taxes. But financial scandal is always hovering in the background.

Mass Suicide

The third and most frightening result of cult abuse is mass suicide. When it happened in Jonestown Guyana in 1979 it was regarded as a freak. It could not happen again, people thought. In the last few years, however, it has happened again, at the Solar Temple in Switzerland and possibly at Waco in Texas, (though that tragedy may have been due to FBI incompetence). Who knows when it might happen again?

In many ways, as we said earlier, there is a predictability about it. Extreme authoritarianism needs at least three things to survive. First it needs an enemy. It has often been said that it is far easier to unite people against something or somebody than for them. History is full of strange alliances, where people of diametrically opposed viewpoints have united against a common foe. One thinks of the alliance of the West and Stalin in the Second World War. The only thing the two parties had in common was a mutual fear of and loathing for the Third Reich. After the end of the war it became apparent just how far apart the sides were, but for the duration their common hostility to Hitler outweighed all else.

Cult leaders are very concerned that they have an enemy. It

makes party discipline so much easier. They have an ever-present threat to speak against, an enemy to watch out for. Consequently it suits them to set up the rest of the world as hostile to them. The fact that the rest of the world may be supremely indifferent to what they are doing is really irrelevant. The cult leader only needs his members to believe that they are hostile. Thus he can convince his group of their divine calling, to root out and oppose the forces of darkness all round them.

Second, authoritarianism needs a purpose. This will usually involve setting up some form of utopia, revolving around the leader and group. The enemy is of course hostile to their divine calling, but they must press on regardless. In some ways it is similar to the aims of Communism, the setting up of a Communist world system. Everything has to be given over to the pursuit of this aim. So in a cult all is presented as being subjugated to this purpose.

This utopian fantasy is held before the group member. One day the world will be united, and it will happen under the Rev. Moon. One day the world will know peace, and it will come about because everyone practises Transcendental Meditation. All the time this goal is just around the corner.

Finally, authoritarianism needs an unthinking obedience. Crack troops in any army are trained to obey orders in any situation and whatever those orders might involve. They must obey unthinkingly and uncritically. Discipline in obedience must be absolute. This is also true within the cults. Once a leader has managed to persuade members to obey him in everything there is little left to test them out on. There is only the final step, the laying down of their lives. No other 'weird obedience' is left to them.

When you put these three things together, the need for an enemy, a purpose, and unthinking obedience you have a lethal mix. This is particularly the case when the group begins to slacken, members leave and momentum dies down. What can the leader do but demand greater and greater sacrifices from the membership? It is all an appalling plot, he will argue. The cause must win, whatever the cost. Little by little there will be mention of the supreme sacrifice. Are the members willing to pay it? Will they go all the way for the cause? Will they be found faithful when the ultimate question is asked of them?

It is all a way of preparing people for the final act of obedience. The apocalyptic scenario is increasingly referred to, the unmentionable begins to be hinted at. By the time the denouement comes, whether by mass deliberate choice, or as part of the leader's intentions, there is a horrible predictability about it. They have been prepared. They can see no other way out.

Notice the way in which a member of the People's Temple in Guyana regarded the mass suicide in Jonestown. These words were recorded in a suicide note he wrote, and they highlight the twisted way of thinking into which Jim Jones had brought them. It is a tragic comment on the psychology of the cults. 'Dad, I see no way out – I agree with your decision – I fear only that without you the world may not make it to communism. For my part I am more than tired of this wretched, merciless planet and the hell it holds for so many masses of beautiful people – thank you the only life I've known.'

Note too the way in which Jim Jones himself encouraged his members to drink the deadly dose of cyanide. They were to see it not as an act of defeat, or surrender, but as their final act of defiance. 'Take the potion like they used to in Ancient Greece and step over quietly. Because we are not committing suicide – it's a revolutionary act.'[9]

Death was not to be seen as defeat but a revolutionary act. It is as though having been led to this point of total submission to the fantasies and follies of the leader, the people should not see suicide as suicide at all. It is the supreme success, the final goal. As Luc Jouret, leader of the Solar Temple in Switzerland put it: 'Liberation is not where human beings think it is. Death can represent an essential stage of life.'

In his book *Shopping for a god*, John Allan makes the point that the exercise of control over a group of people almost inevitably leads to this result. Once all other enemies have been removed, once loyalty has been proved against the enemy without, the only further test of loyalty lies within.

> The escalation of power in [Jim Jones's] case was instructive. The trouble with power is that it always needs opposition to prove itself against, and when it encounters total submission its only recourse is to make new, deeper demands in order to search out the opposition it requires. And so followers are progressively challenged by greater and greater orders involving more and more self-abasement, until the leader has gone as far as he can possibly go. At that point, if he is sick enough, there is only one further, final form of control left: to order his followers to kill themselves and watch while they do it. It is the ultimate abasement, and most cult groups never reach that level. But once, at Jonestown, it happened.[10]

Prophetic words. Since then we have had the horror of Waco, the Solar Temple, and seen the potential horror of Shoko Asahara in Japan. We have seen all too clearly that Jonestown was not a freak, a once-off. It is in many ways the logical conclusion of all authoritarian leadership – although very few, thankfully, actually arrive there. It is the ultimate form of the abuse of power. It is the ultimate test of a member's loyalty and commitment. It is the ultimate proof of the unspeakable vanity and arrogance of leadership.

8

THE DESPAIR OF FRIENDS

What can we do?

For many parents, learning that a son or daughter is caught up in one of the cults is the ultimate nightmare. All the stories, of Jonestown or Waco, fill the thoughts and one can feel utterly helpless. Where does one turn? What can one do? Will the child ever be the same again? Will one ever see them again? Is there any chance of them leaving? If so will they be scarred for life?

I often say to worried parents or friends that the vast majority of those caught up in cults do not remain with them. They have an enormous fall-out rate. Indeed part of the reason for their being so active in proselytising is that there is such a rapid loss that they are constantly looking to replenish numbers. Many are the groups that have at one stage claimed to be the 'fastest-growing' church that are now declining in numbers. When one sees a loved one caught up with such a group it can seem cold comfort to say they will probably come out, but it is worth remembering.

Of course groups have their own way of explaining away their decline in membership. The London Church of Christ at one time boasted that their rapid growth rate proved they were the true church. When numbers began to drop, however, they recognised they needed some new impetus. They called back Douglas Arthur, former head of the London Church, but who had moved on to head up their Commonwealth ministries. For some time they hyped up the visit so that members were aware that something would happen.

In the event what did happen was slightly odd. Instead of

initiating a new recruitment drive, the church decided to cleanse itself. All members were invited to reapply for membership. Those that were not sufficiently engaged in evangelism were refused membership, effectively excommunicated. It was for many – there were 400 in this category – a devastating blow. The church they had believed to be the only true one had told them they were not good enough, and that they had lost their salvation, if they had ever had it.

What was even more extraordinary was the explanation given for this. When a member was asked about this excommunication he replied along the lines of, 'Oh, you mean our revival?' and then proceeded to justify it all on the basis that the church was far better off without them, that they had been dead wood holding up the work of the true believers.

Two things about this are interesting. First, the whole exercise was dressed up in misleading terms. The reapplication for membership simply afforded the leadership an opportunity for pointing the finger at the membership and blaming them. Second, we cannot fail to notice that the whole basis of their original claim to be the true church has changed. Previously it had been that they were larger, or were growing faster than any other. With that mindset, a drop in numbers of 400 would have represented a crushing rejection of that justification. But they had moved the goalposts: no longer was size the mark of the true church – because they were falling in numbers. Now suddenly smaller numbers were the sign of revival.

But what was also revealing was the tacit admission that they were losing members fast. This was due to a combination perhaps of bad publicity, dodgy finances, abusive leadership, and unrealistic expectations. Talking to a former member, who had been baptised by the group in 1987 and had risen to a position of leadership, I was told that of the people who had been baptised that year, at the same time as him, he could only think of about 10 per cent who were still involved with the group. That may well have been an exaggeration, but the fall-out rate is still far larger than any normal church would ever expect in that period of time.

So it is often wise to counsel patience, because for many people membership of a cult is only temporary. We have in our own church people who have been members of the Church of Christ, Jehovah's Witnesses, involved in Transcendental Meditation and numerous other groups. They have found the experience salutary, but not one that has necessarily damaged them for ever.

Let me say also that I have little experience personally in Exit counselling. Although I have met with many ex-members of different groups it tends to be after they have left when they know clearly what has happened, and are coming to terms with it. Moreover I am extremely wary of forcible de-programming. I understand the pressures that drive parents in particular to try such methods and have no wish to criticise them, but I am cautious about it, on grounds of both morality and pragmatics.

First, I do question if it can be right to kidnap people, and force them to face de-programming when they show no desire for it. Maybe in those cases where they have been forcibly detained – and those instances are very few and far between – there is justification. My feeling is, however, that that is a case for the police rather than our trying to take the law into our own hands. For the most part, although they may have been manipulated, those involved in cults are still adult beings who can be advised, warned, and persuaded but should not, I believe, be forced. If we do that, other than in exceptional circumstances, we are playing the same game, indeed a worse game, than the cults. I am unhappy with an 'ends justifies means' argument. I believe there are other means that can be just as successful and do not involve that sort of compromise.

Second, people involved more closely with cults than myself say that that sort of de-programming is not always successful. In those cases where it has worked, it is reckoned that the individual was already showing signs of wanting to come out anyway. What the de-programming did was merely accelerate a process that was already in motion.

But I do believe there will be many times when we will need expert help and counsellors to help those we know to come out of groups. It will not involve force, but it will mean careful, systematic talking over a long period of time, as the individual struggles to regain their identity and come to terms with the errors of the group. For that counselling to be successful there needs to be a willingness on the part of the individual to listen.

But there are certain practical steps anyone can take when they discover that a friend or family member is caught up in a group.

Information

The first thing I would suggest is to be well-informed – get as much information about the group as you possibly can. In the UK there are a number of organisations that can let you know about the different groups, what they believe, who their leaders are, etc. Among them are INFORM – a Government-sponsored organisation that collects information about the new religious movements, as they like to call them. Then there is FAIR (Family Action, Information and Rescue), the Deo Gloria Trust, the Reachout Trust, and the Cults Information Centre. Between them they will probably have details about the group with which you might be concerned.

Being well-informed about a group is the most important place to start. Half-baked and ill-informed prejudice will not help our friends, indeed will probably only drive them further away. If a cult can prove that our accusations about them are false, or our information incorrect, it makes it easier for them to paint their critics as liars, and hence their criticism as invalid.

At the same time most cult members will not know the truth about their organisation. Details about their financial affairs, or any scandals that may have arisen, will carefully be kept from members of the group. I listened recently to a member of one of these groups speaking, and he admitted at the outset that some of us probably knew more about his organisation than he did. A friend who was caught up with the London Church of Christ admitted that the reason he left the church was because he met people who knew more about the church than he did, and who could point out flaws that had been carefully hidden from him;

'My parents called in cult specialists who knew about the group and who challenged me on its teachings. After five minutes talking with them, I knew that something was seriously wrong – but it took me three days of argument to admit that the Church was seriously wrong in its teaching and practice. I left soon afterwards.'[1]

Two things are striking about this. First, it was only because these people knew so much about the church that he felt he had to listen. They could not be written off as ignorant people with an irrational prejudice. Second, although he knew he was wrong it took him three days to admit it. When a person has given up everything to follow a group or leader, it is not easy to eat humble pie and admit that it has all been a ghastly mistake.

If then we want to help our friends caught up in similar groups we need to be informed. Many of these groups have shady reputations, which can easily be discovered by talking to the different agencies, or reading relevant books. Their leaders may have dubious pasts: sometimes thrown out of mainline churches, as Kip McKean of the Boston Church of Christ had been, sometimes with a history of mental instability.

You might discover that although the Book of Mormon is reckoned by Mormons to be 'the most correct of any book on earth' (Joseph Smith Jr, *History of the Church*, 4.461) it has been subject to over three thousand changes since it was written. Moreover no Book of Mormon cities have ever been found, no Book of Mormon names ever been found in New World inscriptions, no mention of Book of Mormon persons, nations, and places have ever been found, and so on.

If you were to study the teaching and history of the Unification Church, you would discover that there are glaring inconsistencies in Sun Myung Moon's account of his life between his 'conversion' experience and his arrival in America, that he has been imprisoned for tax fraud, and that there are outright contradictions in what he says. In *Christianity in Crisis* he states, 'You have heard me speak the Bible. If you believe the Bible, you must believe what I am saying.'[2] But in the *Divine Principle* he declares that the Bible will no longer have any

authority: 'The New Testament words of Jesus and the Holy
Spirit will lose their light . . .' [3]

Uncomfortable truths are often denied or ignored within the
cults. Consequently when we challenge members with them
they often have no answers – indeed there usually are none. But
to do that we need to do our homework first. There is no
substitute for a careful gathering of information.

Communication

The second thing I believe is important is to keep in contact.
Most groups tend to try to split people up from families and
friends. There are a number of reasons for this. The main one
is, I believe, because they know the family will attempt to take
the individual out of the group. They therefore need to present
the family as the enemy, and to ensure that there is as little
contact as possible between the member and his or her family.

They will often use Bible verses to support this behaviour. On
a television programme investigating the activities of the
London Church of Christ, a reporter stopped Fred Scott, leader
of the London Church, outside his car. He was asked why his
group split up families. He immediately opened his Bible to
Luke 14 and read, 'If anyone comes to me and does not hate his
father and mother, his wife and children, his brothers and sisters
– yes, even his own life – he cannot be my disciple.'

This is, of course, a totally fraudulent use of the passage. The
Bible is very strong on the importance of family loyalties – the
command to 'honour your father and mother' is not simply the
first commandment that deals with our human relationships, it
is also the only one combined with a promise 'so that you may
live long in the land' (Exod. 20:12). Jesus was not in any way
trying to overturn the commandment, nor saying that we were
literally to hate those closest to us. It is a hyperbole, a figure of
speech that Jesus often used. He was merely making the point
that we must not allow even the closest of human ties to keep
us from God. Our relationship with God is more important
even than them. The point Jesus is making is not that family ties

are unimportant, but that they are vital. If even our family ties are less important than our relationship to God, how important, therefore, must *that* be.

In fact, as the Bible says often, following Christ should not destroy our human relationships, it should enhance them. How many broken relationships have been restored by Christ. But a friend caught up in this group showed clearly how rather than improving his life and relationships, his new 'faith' actually destroyed them: 'As my intensity and involvement grew, my grades at university fell sharply. I had no time for non-Christian friends. My sense of humour vanished. When challenged on these things by my friends and family, I viewed their remarks as Satanic.'[4]

It is a common and sad story. Group members will often not contact friends and family for a long time at a stretch. It can be extremely painful. It is as though their families have ceased to exist. But we must do all we can to keep the lines of communication open. It can be difficult and costly, but in the long run it is the wisest course of action.

The point is that at some future stage, almost invariably, the individual will find that doubts register in the mind. In my experience when an individual is caught up in a group they are unlikely to listen to anyone else. Any comments will be viewed as hostile, and ignored. Confrontation is rarely the wisest move.

But there will come a time when they begin to ask a few questions, which the groups will be unable or unwilling to answer. At that time they may well want someone to talk to. If you have preserved that friendship they will be willing to talk to you, especially if you have not been judgmental. If, however, you have offended them in the past, they are unlikely to talk to you so readily.

Verification

Following on from that, I think it is wise, when the opportunity presents itself, to restrict oneself to asking questions, seeking to verify from them what has been learnt. The temptation is always to rush in and make all sorts of accusations which may or may not be true. But it is quite possible to win the argument and lose the war. Whenever we attack the church or group our friend will, like as not, go back and talk to their discipler, or group leader, who will probably come up with strong counter-arguments, and will undoubtedly seek to present us as agents of the devil who should not be listened to for any reason.

Far better just to throw the odd pebble in the water and watch the ripples. We may say something like, 'I understand that the Rev. Moon has been in prison for tax fraud – why was that?' or 'A book I was reading claims that the Book of Mormon has undergone some three thousand emendations since it was written – is that really true?' Quite often the person will reject the question, but it may just leave a slight doubt in their minds, which will come back to them at a later stage.

One could liken it to the situation where a young woman brings her latest flame home to meet her parents. The parents are aware that she is deeply in love, but when the couple arrive the parents take an immediate dislike to him. In their minds he is quite unsuitable for their daughter. Perhaps he is the wrong age, has the wrong interests, or maybe he is unstable. But how are they to react?

One option is to make their displeasure clear in no uncertain terms. They can tell her that he is unworthy of her, that she deserves someone better. They could point to all his deficiencies, real or imagined, and tell her she is to give him up immediately. Unfortunately many parents adopt this particular line, and it almost never works. All it manages to do is build a barrier between the girl and her parents so that she will find it difficult to confide in them again. They have effectively asked her to choose between him and them, and she will probably choose him. From that moment onwards their relationship is liable to be a frosty one, if there is any communication at all.

Another option would be to say nothing at all, and pretend that there is no problem. This has the advantage of enabling the relationship between daughter and parents to remain intact, but they would feel they were failing in their duty not to raise any possible cautions. What if she marries the man, and then finds out too late that he is dreadfully unsuited and they have never said anything?

Perhaps the wisest course is simply to raise cautions and questions without being adversarial. One can advise patience, ask pertinent questions about shared interests, how well they know one another, etc. Not that necessarily the girl will immediately see the folly of remaining with him – he might even be the right one for her anyway – but at least the parents will retain her confidence, so that when doubts arise in her mind she will feel able to talk to them about it. At the early stage one of the most important things is keeping the lines of communication open.

A similar plan is probably best when one finds a son or daughter or friend caught up in one of these cults. Steven Hassan, in his book *Combatting Cult and Mind Control*, suggests the following sort of questions that might help in opening up the subject.

How long have you been involved? Are you trying to recruit me?

Most group members see their main role in life as being a recruiter. This is the sort of question therefore that both elicits where they are coming from, and how honest they are prepared to be. The chances are that they will be trying to recruit you, although they might be loath to admit it. They may say, 'No, I would just like to share this with you,' or something similar.

But it is worth noting that the newer a recruit is, the less likely he is to lie. Even if he does lie, Hassan argues, he will be less convincing. If, however, a person has been involved with the group for a good length amount of time, he cannot expect to get away with non-commital answers. He should know the answer to your questions even when he is unwilling to admit it.

Can you tell me the names of all other organisations that are affiliated with this group?

This is again a shrewd question. Moonies will often claim that they are working for world mission, or to unite churches. If they claim this, ask what these churches are. In all probability they do not exist, but you can offer to follow up the answer you are given. It may be too that they will offer the names of front organisations.

The London Church of Christ have claimed that they will work with other Christians for the cause of the gospel: 'It is my sincere desire that there be no quarrelling among those who are sincerely trying to serve Christ in and around London and that a bond of Christian fellowship can develop between us all,' wrote Douglas Arthur in a letter to a worker for the Universities and Colleges Christian Fellowship in 1984.

The only trouble is that they do not believe that any of the other groups or workers belong to Christ at all. They are never satisfied with membership of another church, since only theirs is the true one. They have stated that their policy is never to criticise another church, when in fact they do so constantly, and they publicly rebuke their members for attending other churches.

This of course brings us back to the question of élitism. If they believe that they have the only truth, they will not be working with anyone else, at least not in any meaningful sense.

Who is the top leader? What are his background and qualifications? Does he have any criminal record?
As we saw earlier, the question of leadership is fundamental to an understanding of the work of the cults, yet many of the cult leaders have extremely dubious backgrounds.

Take the case of Sun Myung Moon. While living in North Korea in the 1940s he was sent to jail: 'His followers say that it was because of his anti-communism, while others say it was for bigamy and adultery. A former North Korean army officer who was in prison with Rev. Moon says that Moon received a seven-year sentence for contributing to "social disorder", proclaiming the imminent coming of the second Messiah in Korea.'[5]

There were later accusations of promiscuity and adultery. A leading Presbyterian minister in Seoul claims that members believed they had to receive Moon's blood to receive salvation:

'That blood is ordinarily received by three periods of sexual intercourse.'[6]

The Rev. Moon has since been imprisoned in the US on charges of tax evasion. I suppose you could argue that to fall foul of the law on one occasion could be down to bad luck or injustice, but to be so frequently accused leaves big question marks. I would certainly not want my eternity trusted into the hands of someone with a record like that!

But it is not only the Rev. Moon whose past is dogged by accusations. Kip McKean, founder of the Boston Church of Christ, already had a fairly chequered history by the time he began his group. On one occasion his support at the Memorial Church of Christ in Houston had been terminated because: '... Brother McKean has brought unbiblical practices, peculiar language and subtle, deceitful doctrines to Charleston ...'[7]

One could look at the leadership of many of these groups, and find strange details about their past. Embarrassing events are given a gloss, or covered up altogether. For instance, Joseph Smith's marriage to Emma Smith in 1827 followed their elopement, because her father had refused to give the marriage his blessing. The official reason given for this in Smith's autobiography was the persecution Smith experienced after his vision. However Fawn Brodie, in her biography of Smith, *No Man Knows My History*, shows through documentary evidence that 'the real reason for Mr Hale's refusal was that at this time Smith's only occupation was that of digging for money with the help of a "peepstone" into which he would gaze to determine the location of the treasure.'[8]

One could go on about the backgrounds of Jim Jones, or David Koresh, or about how David Berg's first pastorate ended in acrimony which gave him a permanent contempt for organised religion. But what is significant is that the membership is likely to know absolutely nothing about these events.

If you look into the past you will frequently find therein the seeds of destruction. It is always worth discovering the religious background of any leader. Where there is a pattern of irresponsible behaviour, or a refusal to submit to authority, or maybe a sense of isolation, then there is cause for concern.

What does your group believe?

Deception lies at the heart of the cults, and this is never more apparent than in their recruiting. Their aim is not to pass on the teaching of the group, but to get you to one of their meetings. Even then it can be some time before you ever get to the bottom of what their message actually is. In the meantime they want so to overwhelm you with their love, warmth, and friendliness that you commit yourself to the group before you understand their teaching fully, and when you do finally realise you are too deeply entrenched to get out.

Ask them what they believe. How does their teaching differ from that of othodox Christianity? Ask them where traditional Christianity has gone wrong – not in its practice but its teaching. Ask them to explain, as simply and clearly as they can, what the group stands for. Any legitimate group should be able to summarise its central beliefs, while destructive of abusive cults will not want to do so.

Does your group believe that the ends justify the means? Is deception allowed?

This is again one of the defining marks of the cults and it is worth investigating. Are there ever occasions when it would be right to lie or deceive for the benefit of the group or in recruiting for the group?

We know of course that there are many. But it is interesting to ask if this is ever the case, particularly if the person has either been shy about telling you the nature of their beliefs, or even told you lies. You might ask a Moonie why they operate under so many different names. Is the Unification Church not good enough? You could ask a member of the London Church of Christ why, when they had been banned from the London School of Economics, they then operated under two totally different names.

What are members expected to do once they join? Will they have to quit school, work, donate money, cut themselves off from friends and family?

Most cult members will, of course, say that the reason they may have left their homes or careers or college courses was because they wanted to give themselves to the group, rather than because they were under pressure to do so. They will probably say that the cult makes few, if any, demands upon a member. Any commitment is self-motivated.

But it is a question that can make a cult member uncomfortable and defensive. So perhaps you can ask further, what the member did when he joined the group, how many of the group do have ordinary jobs, do not live in the group's houses. Is the group member now expected to make big donations? Does he still have a job?

It can be useful to ask further questions about the group's use of money. Have they ever seen a copy of their group's accounts? If so, how detailed are they? Some groups issue accounts that really say nothing, and are incapable of true interpretation. Ask about the amounts of money earned by the leadership. How does it compare with that earned by members?

One lady who used to be fundraiser for the Mormon Church asked to see the accounts of the church. She was duly refused on the basis that she ought to 'have faith in' how they would use the money. A former member of the London Church of Christ, who knew the state of the accounts, advised the leadership on a number of occasions that the financial affairs were out of order, only to be told that they were in hand. While he was with the group, they were never sorted out, although he suspected members were being paid cash-in-hand and the earnings not declared.

Is your group under suspicion? If people are critical of your group, what are their objections?

Most cults are the object of suspicion by the outside world. But this question will elicit just how much the member is aware of these suspicions. For the most part cults try to keep such information from the members, but they will be aware of the accusations of being a cult. They may well therefore reply with, 'Some people think we are a cult, and that we are brainwashed. But do I look brainwashed?'

Hassan says that whenever someone says that to him, his immediate reply is, 'Oh, how are people supposed to look if they are brainwashed?' and the cult member has no answer.

But members will probably not be aware of other criticisms of the group. Such information is kept from them, and they will be allowed no contact with former members.

How do you/does the group feel about former members? Does the group impose restrictions on meeting with former members? Have you talked with any about their reasons for leaving?

Reaction to those who have left the group is often the clearest sign of a cult. They are attacked, abused, and cut off from the group – any contact with them is forbidden. This would never happen with a legitimate group. We have people who leave our church, some to join other churches, others to leave church altogether. When these latter go it is sad. But we would not dream of making them pariahs, or forbidding anyone to have contact with them. Indeed we would want to draw them back into Christian things if we could.

Not so with the cults. Perhaps because they know that there is too much to hide they may forbid any contact with ex-members. They will say that it is because they have given themselves over to Satan, and are beyond help. In reality it is because when a member talks to an ex-member they may discover the real truth about the group and be tempted to leave themselves.

What are the three things you like least about the group and the leader?

No group is perfect, no church is perfect, and if you were to ask members of most churches they would soon be able to tell you what they thought was wrong with their church! Perhaps the preaching is too long and boring, or not meaty enough. They will probably find something wrong with the music – too traditional or too modern. It could be the form of services, or the pastor, but it would not be too difficult for them to find something. They may not be overly critical but it is extremely unlikely that anyone would think their church was perfect.

If you asked a member of one of the cults about the faults within the group, however, they would not know what to say. All criticism is discouraged, and to be asked to express any critical comment is to be asked the impossible. As likely as not they will say that there is nothing with which they can find fault.

There are only two reasons why a member might think their group perfect. The first is that they are frightened to express criticism because it shows a bad spirit, and a lack of reverence. They are not used to asking questions or expressing contrary opinions and so it is an impossible question. They are conditioned to believe that all criticism is of the devil, or whatever enemy they believe in. The other is that they genuinely believe that the group is perfect, and the leaders in particular. Now no group can be perfect, and this is a sure sign that they are not really in any emotional state to hear criticism. They are so wrapped up in it that everything is perfect and nothing could be wrong.

On one occasion I recall trying to argue with a Moonie about the errors of the Rev. Moon's teaching, and after about thirty fairly fruitless minutes of trying to understand what he was saying, he suddenly exploded. It was one of the most disturbing things I have ever seen. He quite simply flipped. It was as though he was unable to comprehend that Moon and his teaching could in any way be wrong, and so, like a little child – which in effect he had become – he threw a tantrum. It was as though his world was in danger of collapsing, and he just could not face it. At the end of the encounter I felt deflated. I may have won the argument, for what it was worth, but it had not done any good. I had only proved myself, in his eyes, to be an enemy of the truth.

The best policy, then, is to hold fire until such time as the person is able and willing to listen. When they want answers to basic questions, and are not getting any within the group, perhaps then the opportunity will present itself. Until then the best plan is to stay in touch, learn all one can about the group, ask the odd question, and wait.

As a Christian one must pray, for ultimately it is a spiritual issue. It is almost impossible to argue a person out of the cults until they are ready to listen. But as we pray, we may find the person will show an increasing frustration with the group, and uneasiness. At that moment we need to be ready – both in such a position of trust that they will listen, but also with the necessary information.

9

THE DANGER OF PRAGMATISM

What do we learn?

'Let anyone who thinks that he stand, take heed lest he fall.'

1 Corinthians 10:12

From all that has been said so far it should be apparent that there is no clear dividing line between those groups we regard as mainstream and those we see as abusive. Indeed many of the faults found in those we describe as cults are latent in some recognised churches. So those of us who would call ourselves Christians have hard lessons to learn if we are to avoid those dangers. What are those lessons?

Churches have a responsibility to teach and nurture. That has always been and should remain the prime calling of Christian ministry. Our aim is to 'proclaim Christ, admonishing and teaching everyone with all wisdom, so that we may present everyone perfect in Christ' (Col. 1:28). Of course many of the groups cited in this book would claim the same objective. It is in the working out of that objective that groups go astray, however, and it is here that ordinary Christian churches should beware.

My former vicar knows it as the principle of the angle. Heresy can be like two lines almost parallel to one another, moving from the same point only a degree apart. Initially they seem to run together, but as time goes on they gradually become more obviously apart until eventually they are miles away from each other.

A Jim Jones, a David Koresh, or a David Berg can seem to all intents and purposes part of the mainline Christian Church. He can be accepted and welcomed within church groups. He can be respected, admired, and even envied by other Christian leaders for his dynamism and his success. But somewhere, even at the outset, the faultlines are apparent to the discerning, faultlines that will ultimately lead to disaster. The question is, how can churches and church leaders protect themselves from going down that road, and how can we recognise it and warn against it when we see it in others?

I have no desire to enter into a heresy hunt – they do not have a particularly distinguished history. On the other hand if we can help one another to recognise these faults before they become too major, much pain will be avoided. I would like to pose certain questions that I believe need to be asked of any church or church leader if it is to be protected.

The demise of the Nine O'Clock Service in Sheffield has alerted us that the danger is a real and present one. It is not enough, I believe, to state that this was simply a matter of an individual taking upon himself a power he should not have done, and abusing it. It is not enough to say it was only about power – the idea was great, the individual wrong – as so many have since claimed. The writing was on the wall long before it transpired that the leaders were abusing members.

So what can the Church learn from these disasters? How can we recognise the seeds of trouble before it all blows up in our faces? Given that false teaching and false teachers will always be with us, how can we be more alert? I would like to mention a number of areas where we need to be especially wary.

Truth

Our attitude towards the cults will inevitably be affected by our understanding of truth. If we follow the modern mindset that says that there are many truths, and each person's perception is of equal validity, then we can have little quarrel at least with the teaching of the cults. I cannot be content to do that. The

Christian is convinced that there is a body of teaching that God has handed down to us, and we are not free to take or leave it as we choose. Indeed the New Testament has many things to say about how we are to guard, and fight for the truth (2 Tim. 1:14, Jude 3). God has revealed His truth, supremely in Christ, and in the Bible, and we cannot play fast and loose with it.

And yet within the Church today there is a notable lack of confidence in the truth. Doctrine is not widely taught, or accepted. There is a widespread belief that people just will not accept the old, old story any more. It is too incredible. Therefore we have to find something that they *can* believe. Truth is thus determined not by revelation but by what is deemed to be acceptable. So the gospel is determined by what the market wants – or at least what certain people deem the market to want.

This subtle shift is seen clearly in the nature of the truth or gospel we present. The traditional Christian gospel has stated that all human beings are sinful and stand in need of forgiveness. This forgiveness is not something that we can earn, but is freely available through the death of Christ on the cross. Once we receive that forgiveness and new life we are called to live lives of holiness.

Such a gospel will not do for today, it is argued. Our society has become obsessed with the self, and it is demeaning and humiliating for the self to learn that it is sinful. In any case we only fail or fall short because of the influence of others around us, our parents, society, and so on. In other words it is not my fault. Indeed the reverse is true. I am not a sinner, but a victim. Listen to the words of a famous and respected Christian teacher in the US: 'I don't think anything has been done in the name of Christ and under the banner of Christianity that has proved more destructive to human personality and hence counterproductive to the evangelism enterprise than the often crude, uncouth and unchristian strategy of attempting to make people aware of their lost and sinful condition.'[1]

Since therefore we are not sinners but victims, it is no longer forgiveness that we need, but healing – hence countless books on inner healing, healing the memories, etc. And what is our eventual goal? It is no longer holiness, but the much more pleasing one of wholeness. Here then we have a totally different gospel for our self-centred age. For sin, read sickness. For forgiveness, read healing. For holiness, read wholeness. And of course it is a more attractive gospel. It tells me that I am OK, that if I have my weaknesses, it is always somebody else's fault. And my great goal in life is to fulfil myself, to be whole, to be me, to do what I want.

As an illustration of this there have been a number of very sad scandals within different parts of the Church in recent years – instances of child sexual abuse, for example. They have rocked the Church, and damaged the faith of many ordinary church-going Christians. But what is so fascinating is to see how these scandals are dealt with. In almost every instance the first thing that happens is that the guilty person is sent to see a counsellor, or psychiatrist. Why? Because they are regarded as being not sinful, but sick. There has to be a reason why he or she behaved like this, other than the obvious one of ordinary human sin. The modern gospel has little room for sin, so it is conveniently changed.

One problem with this is that there is no evidence that people cannot believe the old biblical gospel. Indeed the churches that believe it are often very full. But, much more fundamentally, we cannot allow our gospel to be determined by what others may or may not accept. The gospel is a trust given to us by Christ, and we simply do not have the liberty to change it. We are not to be a consumer-led organisation. In this instance the customer is *not* always right. Yet there is within the church today a craze for market research, endless surveys are done, all to discover why people do not go to church, or find Christianity irrelevant. It is as though as soon as we know the reason for this we can adjust accordingly. But too often it is not our presentation we end up adjusting – and in many cases it does need adjusting – but the product itself, the message of the gospel. All we show by this is that we do not really trust the gospel at all.

What also happens when as a Church we develop a lack of

confidence in the truth is that we are more liable to fall for error. Being unfamiliar or superficial in our understanding of truth, we do not recognise error when it comes in. We do not have the theological capacity to judge a new teaching. Yet the best way to defend ourselves against false teaching is to be fully conversant with the truth. Walter Martin uses an illustration from the banking world:

> The American Banking Association ... each year sends hundreds of bank tellers to Washington in order to teach them to detect counterfeit money ... It is most interesting that during the entire two weeks of the training programme, no teller touches counterfeit money. Only the original passes through his hands. The reason for this is that the ABA is convinced that if a man is thoroughly familiar with the original, he will not be deceived by a counterfeit bill, no matter how much like the original it appears.'[2]

The Christian world is susceptible to false teaching precisely because it has such a shaky grasp upon the truth. The Apostle Paul states in Ephesians:

> It was [Christ] who gave some to be apostles, some to be prophets, some to be evangelists, and some to be pastors and teachers, to prepare God's people for works of service, so that the body of Christ can be built up until we all reach unity in the faith and in the knowledge of the Son of God and become mature, attaining to the whole measure of the fullness of God. Then we will no longer be infants, tossed back and forth by the waves, and blown here and there by every wind of teaching and by the cunning and craftiness of men in their deceitful scheming. (Eph. 4:11–14)

God's remedy for false teaching, His protection for His people, is sound Bible teaching. The point is that so much of the false teaching of today is simply the old heresies under another guise. They are still concerned with the incarnation, with authority, with Christian lifestyle, with the meaning of freedom. If only we knew our Bibles better, perhaps we would recognise heresy more easily. This brings us to another lesson, which springs from this lack of confidence in the truth.

Presentation

If we have less confidence in the truth as presented in the Bible, it will affect the way in which we present our faith. We will appeal less to the mind and human reason, and more to the heart and emotions.

It is no surprise therefore that what we see so often is a correspondingly greater emphasis now on experience. What matters is no longer what we believe, but what we experience. One of the most powerful movements in this country over the last eighteen months has been that of the so-called Toronto Blessing. Many churches and church leaders have adopted this as the sign of revival or refreshment. All are encouraged to share in this blessing. But if you analyse what is actually being taught, it really boils down to experience – you have to have 'the blessing'. Those who do not have it are often regarded as second class, their Christian lives dry and powerless.

At the same time there has been a corresponding lack of teaching of the Bible. All sorts of biblical justifications for the Blessing are brought in, which transparently have nothing to do with it. The Bible is used at times dishonestly. What transpires is a theology that lays itself wide open to abuse. Perhaps some parts of the Church have lost faith and confidence in the message, and feel that an experience is both more attractive and relevant. But in this not only has the emphasis moved from truth to experience, it has also moved from God to us. It is not what God says that is the key, but what I experience. It is a me-centred message fro a me-centred age.

On two occasions in recent months I have talked with people who have claimed an evangelical faith, but whose understanding of the gospel was radically different. In their view the aim of Christian ministry has been to help people to recognise the spirituality within themselves. That is not the New Testament understanding of the gospel. The gospel comes not to affirm the spirituality we already possess but to change it. It is not a me-centred message, but a God-centred one. It does not tell us that we are OK as we are, it tells us we need to change – but that God can change us.

We need therefore to recognise that our understanding of the gospel will inevitably affect our presentation. If we believe that everyone has a certain spirituality within them that needs to be released, then our aim will not be to teach them – after all, the spirituality they already possess is valid in itself – but to encourage them. We may well try to do this in special services, for instance.

If, on the other hand, we believe that the understanding of God a person naturally possesses is inadequate, even wrong, then we will try to teach them. We recognise that they need to know and respond to the truth. Therefore the most important part of any meeting or service will be the teaching. Whatever the other ingredients of a service, people must be enabled to hear and respond to truth as it is presented. They need to understand God. When it comes to teaching people we have to use words and speech, and appeal to the mind – because it is our thinking that needs to be changed, not our emotions. Of course spiritual truth is understood by the Spirit speaking to our spirits, yet in the New Testament this is through the mind: 'Not so did you learn Christ . . . pray that I may make it clear, as I ought to speak'.

So often Christian meetings are run with the express aim of creating a certain effect, making it psychologically and emotionally easier for people to respond to whatever message is being proclaimed, when in all honesty the proclamation is at best inadequate and at worst plain wrong. Far more time is spent on the presentation than on the message. Or, put another way, the medium has become more important than the message.

Again and again I find programmes being advertised, courses being marketed, on the grounds that they *work*: it is not whether it is a clear or faithful presentation of the message, but whether it is effective. Indeed the message may be compromised if it is perhaps a little unpalatable.

I wonder if it is here that the most important lesson of some of the recent disasters to befall the Western Church needs to be grasped. We have tended to argue that cults are about the abuse of power. To a large extent they are. But that is surely not enough. In saying that, we are effectively saying that it does not matter what is presented provided it is done decently. What inevitably ensues is that nobody will ask questions about content as long as a particular programme seems to be successful. Surely one of the problems of the Nine O'Clock Service was that nobody dared touch it because it seemed to be working. Young people were drawn in, the church became relevant. Yet all the time, despite protestations to the contrary, the theology and the message were very far from biblical truth.

When young women dressed only in bikinis are seen to dance erotically on stage it is seen as OK because it is experimental, and because it 'works'. But what about the scriptural injunction not to give even the appearance of sin (1 Thess. 5:22)? What about the dangers of leading others into sin? (Could it really be argued, with any honesty, that suggestive dancing would *not* lead others, at the very least, into impure thoughts?) And were the leaders involved really that sanctified that they were not liable themselves to be led into sin? 'Let anyone who thinks that he stands take heed lest he fall' (1 Cor. 10:12). Well, as time has tragically shown, they were not. But why should anyone have believed that they were? Was it not both unbelievable arrogance and foolish naïvety?

Unfortunately nobody, or very few, dared touch it because it was seen to be successful. The great god of success reared its head again. To criticise such services was seen as criticising the Lord's anointed. Sadly, the Church – and I am very much a part of that Church, so cannot claim to be innocent – has desired success above all. In some ways we are only reaping the harvest we have sown. Because we have seen 'reaching' people, or 'relating' to them as our supreme concern, we have fallen for easy short cuts.

But it goes a good deal farther than that. The main emphasis of the NOS, and of many other such groups, lies not on truth as such, but presentation and experience. What matters is not so much correct theology – which is seen as boring and arid – but on our experience of God. Consequently ideas are brought in from anywhere, if they will lead to a deeper experience. The flirtation of the NOS with the teaching of Matthew Fox should have been enough to alert any orthodox Christian to the fact that they were moving, or already had moved, a vast distance from traditional Christianity in belief, not just in practice.

The irony is that the one protection the NOS would have had against that heresy creeping in, with all its attendant dangers, was precisely the sort of clear, systematic and careful Bible teaching they seem to have rejected. What was so striking about the NOS was that it earned the respect of people from across the theological spectrum, precisely because truth as such was less important than experience.

Interestingly, in the immediate aftermath of the NOS debacle there were any number of commentators who were claiming that it was simply a matter of abuse of power, but that the experiment was valid. The theology was fine, it is just that it was abusive. Within the Church, however, there were many who disagreed. It was not just the abuse – for them the whole concept was flawed. It was not, as so many have rushed to announce, just a cultural thing. Sexual dancing at a service is not just a matter of a certain dance-club culture, it is a matter of sin.

There is a feeling about today – one which I believe is of immense danger to the Church at large – that because our age is largely one that looks for experience, the Church must meet that need by offering an experience. Many of the movements within the Church today stem from this deep desire to give an experience. Commentators point out that until the Church meets this need it will continue to fail. A respected Catholic writer said this:

The Church of England has not historically associated with extremes of religious expression . . . yet this very moderation is perhaps inadequate to meet the present need for feeling – for ecstasy ... Reason there must be in the tradition of religious faith – but what touches the heart, what moves the spirit, what makes people feel that sense of the beautiful and the sublime and the divine, must be there too if the ministry is to reach out to people, and particularly young people.[3]

It seems to me this is a very dangerous position to adopt for two reasons. First it assumes that unless we can offer people an experience they will not listen. What about truth? Has that no part to play? Have we so imbibed the ethos of the culture that we cannot have any confidence in truth? Is the only arbiter of truth now to be experience? Can young people only accept truth if it is to be accompanied by flashing lights, loud music, and video images? Are we really saying that the truth of forgiveness and eternal life, and the resurrection of the dead, has no relevance for people unless it is accompanied by, indeed preceded by, experience? When a member of my family or a friend dies, it is not an experience I seek but truth. What has happened to them? What hope have they?

But second, does that mean that the presentation of truth can have no experiential impact? There is a suggestion that unless in some way we appeal to people's emotions then they will never respond to the gospel. But it is never our techniques that bring a person to faith, it is a sovereign work of God's Spirit. By seeking to make an appeal primarily to people's emotions we are effectively saying that God cannot really be trusted to do that work. Again we come back to Paul's words in 2 Corinthians 4:2 'We have renounced secret and shameful ways; we do not use deception, nor do we distort the word of God. On the contrary, by setting forth the truth plainly we commend ourselves to every man's conscience in the sight of God.'

The concern of Christians is to make the truth as plain as they can, and leave the consequences to God. It is not that we are to despise modern culture, or use old language, but that we are never to allow the medium to become more important than the message. It is the message itself that has the power, and it does not depend upon our manipulation. 'I am not ashamed of the gospel, because it is the power of God for the salvation of everyone who believes' (Rom. 1:16).

Ultimately, succumbing to pragmatism or technique to put across the message is to show lack of confidence in the message itself. If one looks at many so-called gospel presentations today they are long on gimmicks, on techniques, but very short on content. And in the end it will backfire on us. We will only be left with a Church that is superficial, liable to be blown one way and another by every new fad and teaching. This brings us naturally to the next area.

Evangelism

As we noted earlier, one of the marks of the cults is their commitment to recruiting. A member's main responsibility is often as either recruiter or fundraiser, usually both. It is in the exercise of that responsibility that they go so far wrong.

Now of course the final command of Christ was 'Go, therefore and make disciples of all nations'. Christians cannot escape the responsibility and privilege of evangelism. After all, if God has done all this for us, should we not want others to know it too? But how is this responsibility to be exercised?

We have already touched on this when we looked at our presentation of truth. There is an alarming pragmatism about so much that passes for evangelism today. We are concerned not so much with whether a presentation is entirely faithful to the truth, but whether it will get results. But how does this manifest itself?

First there may be a desire to *avoid unpalatable truths*. We have seen how the cults will often cloak their message for fear of putting people off. They will deny who they are, and what they really believe. They will preach a gospel that they think people will want to hear. They will appeal to the mood of the age.

But is the Church so very different? Obviously we believe that the gospel is the answer to human aspirations, but there are times when we allow the gospel to be defined and conditioned almost entirely by the secular world. Does the world hate the very idea of sacrifice or commitment? Is the thought of self-discipline repugnant? Well, we will not mention them. Does the world find the idea of the uniqueness of Christ offensive? Then we will not mention it. Is the thought of the judgment anathema to the contemporary mind? Then we will leave out the idea of God's wrath and instead concentrate on His love. In a recent survey conducted among American Christians, it was discovered that '7 out of 10 . . . deny the possibility that pain or suffering could be a means of becoming a better, more mature individual . . . 3 out of 10 agree that "Nothing in life is more important than having fun and being happy." '

Presumably that is the gospel they are being taught today, and no doubt it is popular. But it is not true. The desire to avoid offence is very deep in many of us. We desperately want to be accepted and to please. But in the process the gospel is compromised. It may not be for the same reasons as in the cults, it may not be to gain attention or followers for ourselves, but the temptation is the same.

Alongside this is the pressure to *affirm unbiblical standards*. By this I mean that just as we leave out bits in the gospel that the world finds unpalatable, so we are also in danger of including bits that are not in the gospel, but which the world finds palatable.

It may be an attitude towards wealth and health. In the last thirty years there has been an inordinate focus in the churches on these two areas. We have been told that the Church needs a change in world-view, that we need to believe God for more, that we are faithless. But what we are being told to expect in the Christian life are things that the New Testament never expects of us. Christ never calls us to be rich and healthy. He calls us to be sacrificial and holy. But somehow that is not quite so attractive to the twentieth century, Western mind.

It may be in the area of sexual morality. There has been an enormous change in attitudes towards biblical standards in the last fifty years and the Church reflects that. The idea that the

God-given standard for sexual behaviour is faithfulness within marriage and celibacy outside of it is regarded as *passé*. So we conveniently move the goalposts: now we are told there are many different models and all that really matters is integrity. The world will not buy our standards – so we change them.

Lastly there is the temptation to *apply unwarranted pressure*. The cults frequently use emotional and psychological pressure to recruit, but again it is not beyond the Church of today to resort to similar tactics. It may be heavily-hyped services, over-glamorous testimonies, weekends away, and peer pressure. We may never allow an individual the time or space to think for themselves.

We need to remember that whenever we do that, we are trying to do God's work for Him. It is not our efforts that will win people to Christ, it is the work of His Spirit, because it is not human effort that prevents the work of the gospel, but Satan.

And even if our gospel is veiled, it is veiled to those who are perishing. The god of this age has blinded the minds of unbelievers, so that they cannot see the light of the gospel of the glory of Christ, who is the image of God ... For God, who said, 'Let light shine out of darkness,' made his light shine in our hearts to give us the light of the knowledge of the glory of God in the face of Christ. (2 Cor. 4:3–4, 6)

Authority

Abusive churches or cults centre around a particular under-standing of leadership, authority, and how it is understood and exercised. At the heart of every cult there is a leader or leadership with an unhealthy authority over the lives and beliefs of the members. Without an abusive leadership those we know as cults would simply be unorthodox religions. It is the unhealthy exercise of authority that so often causes the prob-lems. We cannot avoid, therefore, turning the spotlight on our understanding of leadership. When we see the appalling way in which authority is exercised and abused within the cults it is a timely warning to Christian leaders.

It is a warning about *infallibility*. No Christian leader is infallible, since infallibility rightly belongs only to God and His Word. Therefore we must always treat claims to special anointing or special knowledge with great scepticism. So often it is when a congregation accepts that their leader is somehow uniquely knowledgeable, and allows them to do their thinking for them that they open themselves up to abuse. It is when they quote him about any subject, or defer to him in all matters, that they cross the line. Beware of new revelations!

Paul warned the early Christians that they should not accept even his word when it went against the gospel he had taught them. 'But even if we or an angel from heaven should preach a gospel other than the one we preached to you, let him be eternally condemned!' (Gal. 1:8).

Our supreme authority is and must remain the Bible. All leaders must submit themselves to the Bible, and never set themselves either above it, or as sole true interpreters of it. For any one individual to set themselves up as being the only true representative of that God, or for an individual to claim that they are the only true prophet, or that they have been given a new revelation that no one else has received, is to fly in the face of New Testament teaching. Christ is our head, and His teaching our only infallible guide.

Wherever we find the teachings of a particular leader quoted more often than the Bible, or their books read more avidly, we need to beware. Again and again we find that the teachings of X on the Bible – and often the most fanciful of interpretations or loosest of explanations – have taken the place of Scripture.

Whenever we find some new experience or new discovery, or new teaching being writ large in churches or Christian bookshops as though this is the answer to our problems, again we need to tread very carefully to ensure it does not take the place of the Bible. Whenever we engage in the establishing of Christian heroes or heroines, set leaders up on a pedestal, treat them as demigods without recognising that their hearts are as sinful as ours, we risk being deceived or disappointed by them.

It is also a warning about *accountability*. When a church and church leader cut themselves off from outside accountability, they can begin to believe their own publicity, and become a law unto themselves. There must be some built-in accountability. The trouble is that so often a group so believes in its own uniqueness that it is unwilling to submit itself in that way. For instance, how can the London Church of Christ make itself accountable when it recognises nobody else as being Christian? Accountability is all part of the biblical command to 'submit to one another' (Eph. 5:21).

It is a warning about *loyalty*. What sort of commitment is expected of members to the church? Is commitment to the church placed before, or even seen as synonymous with, commitment to Christ? How easily Christian leaders, particularly dynamic, charismatic (in a non-colloquial sense) leaders attract people to themselves rather than Christ. It may be the youth leader, or the young pastor, but the danger is in drawing people to oneself rather than Christ. That is always the sign of the false teacher. We need to mark well the words of Paul in Galatians 4:

Those people are zealous to win you over, but for no good. What they want is to alienate you from us, *so that you may be zealous for them*. It is fine to be zealous, provided the purpose is good, and to be so always and not just when I am with you. My dear children, for whom I am again in the pains of childbirth until Christ is formed in you, how I wish I could be with you now and change my tone, because I am perplexed about you! (Gal. 4:17–20, my italics).

How painful is the contrast between Paul's attitude and that of the false teachers. Indeed Paul elsewhere was able to say that his own reputation was of no concern, provided the gospel was being proclaimed (Phil. 1:15–18). Beware of empire-builders!

It is a warning too about *humility*. There is a fundamental arrogance about cult leaders that is so different from the servant spirit of Christ and the early disciples. The true leader is a servant, and does not set himself above the group members, or cut himself off from them. 'He who would be great among you must be your servant.'

It is a warning about *manipulation*. How easily we manipulate, or seek to control people when the gospel seeks to set them free. In Colossians 2, Paul speaks of the effects that the false teachers were having upon their followers.

> See to it that no one takes you captive through hollow and deceptive philosophy, which depends on human tradition and the basic principles of this world rather than on Christ. . . . Therefore do not let anyone judge you by what you eat or drink, or with regard to a religious festival, a New Moon celebration or a Sabbath day. These are a shadow of the things that were to come; the reality, however, is found in Christ. Do not let anyone who delights in false humility and the worship of angels disqualify you for the prize. Such a person goes into great detail about what he has seen, and his unspiritual mind puffs him up with idle notions. He has lost connection with the Head, from whom the whole body, supported and held together by its ligaments and sinews, grows as God causes it to grow. (Col. 2:8, 16–19)

Notice the power of those three verbs: false teaching will be liable to enslave – 'takes you captive' – to 'judge' and to 'disqualify'. Whenever our teaching or exercise of authority brings people into that sort of bondage there is real cause for concern.

Elitism

There is a strong tendency within many churches to regard only their group as being correct. Nobody else is quite good enough, sound enough or spiritual enough. It can reflect itself in a partisan spirit which is always comparing itself, favourably of course, with others. Yet often these factions are caused not by fundamental disagreements of doctrine, but matters of taste or secondary importance. It was a party spirit that split apart the church at Corinth:

> My brothers, some from Chloe's household have informed me that there are quarrels among you. What I mean is this: One of you says, 'I follow Paul'; another, 'I follow Apollos'; another, 'I follow Cephas'; still another 'I follow Christ.' Is Christ divided?' (1 Cor. 1:11–13a).

This élitism causes an us-and-them attitude, whereby those not with us are regarded as being at best second-class. It builds a church with no fringe, and as has been said before, 'a church with no fringe is a cult'.

Finance

Since it is in the area of finance that so many of the cults fall down it is worth stating that Christian churches should be above reproach in the way they handle money. The congregation should know what the financial affairs of the church are, and how the money is spent. It can often be a matter of frustration that so much time at church meetings tends to be taken up with discussing finance, but it is preferable to conducting financial affairs in private. The way a church uses money is not a bad indication of its spiritual state. Integrity and generosity in this area is of vital importance.

Thus it follows that the annual accounts of any church should be open for public inspection, so that people can see clearly that money is used wisely. Equally there should be no long emotional pleas for money. Giving should be seen simply as part of a person's natural Christian commitment.

There is much more that could be said. But the warnings to both pastors and members are clear enough. For members there is the real responsibility of acting like the Bereans of Acts 17, who 'received the message with great eagerness and examined the Scriptures every day to see if what Paul said was true' (Acts 17:11). Church members cannot and must not devolve responsibility for thought onto their pastors and teachers. They must be prepared to ask questions, and make constructive criticism if they are to avoid being led astray. A church that never questions will end up being exploited.

Equally there is a big challenge for any of us who are pastors. We must not betray the God-given trust that we have received. There should be an integrity, an openness, and a consistency about both our lives and our teaching that can withstand scrutiny and questioning. We are to 'watch our life and doctrine closely' (1 Tim. 4:16), not to look for short cuts, and remember that it is perseverance that ultimately will count. 'Persevere in them, because if you do, you will save both yourself and your hearers.'

The word of the LORD came to me: 'Son of man, prophesy against the shepherds of Israel; prophesy and say to them: "This is what the Sovereign LORD says: Woe to the shepherds of Israel who only take care of themselves! Should not shepherds take care of the flock? You eat the curds, clothe yourselves with the wool and slaughter the choice animals, but you do not take care of the flock. You have not strengthened the weak or healed the sick or bound up the injured. You have not brought back the strays or searched for the lost. You have ruled them harshly and brutally. So they were scattered because there was no shepherd, and when they were scattered they became food for all the wild animals.

Therefore, you shepherds, hear the word of the LORD: As surely as I live, declares the Sovereign LORD, because my flock lacks a shepherd and so has been plundered and has become food for all the wild animals, and because my shepherds did not search for my flock but cared for themselves rather than for my flock, therefore, O shepherds, hear the word of the LORD: This is what the Sovereign LORD says: I am against the shepherds and will hold them accountable for my flock. I will remove them from tending the flock so that the shepherds can no longer feed themselves. I will rescue my flock from their mouths, and it will no longer be food for them.

I myself will search for my sheep and look after them . . . I will rescue them from all the places where they were scattered on a day of clouds and darkness . . . I myself will tend my sheep and have them lie down, declares the Sovereign LORD. I will search for the lost and bring back the strays. I will bind up the injured and strengthen the weak, but the sleek and the strong I will destroy. I will shepherd the flock with justice.

. . . Then they will know that I, the LORD their God, am with them and that they, the house of Israel, are my people, declares the Sovereign LORD. You my sheep, the sheep of my pasture, are people, and I am your God, declares the Sovereign LORD." ' (Ezek. 34)

Points to Consider

1. How is your church governed?

The New Testament answer to such a question is clear. It is Jesus Christ who is the head of the Church: 'Christ is the head of the church, his body, of which he is the Saviour' (Eph. 5:23). Equally Christ is the only mediator between us and God: 'For there is one God and one mediator between God and men, the man Christ Jesus.'

What is the leadership structure? How accountable is it? To what authority is your church answerable? Is there a placing of leaders on pedestal?

Galatians 1:8–9.

2. How is your church controlled?

What sort of control is exercised on ordinary members? Are they allowed to disagree?

1 Peter 5:2–5; 2 Corinthians 7:2.

3. How is your church defined?

Does it have a fringe? Is there a sense in which everyone is clearly in or out? How exclusive/élitist is it?

James 2:1–7.

4. How does your church recruit?

Is the gospel presented clearly, simply and without histrionics? Do the teachers attempt to deceive or distort the gospel?

2 Corinthians 4:1–6.

5. How is your church taught?

How clearly is the Bible taught? Does the authority come from the Bible or from people's interpretation of the Bible? Or from people's personal experience? Or from their revelations?

Galatians 1:8–9.

Is truth placed at a high premium?

6. How is your church advertised?

Is there a note of triumphalism? A note of comparing selves with others? An element of competitiveness?

2 Corinthians 12:1–10.

7. How does your church raise/use money?

Does it show integrity and generosity?

1 Timothy 6:3–10.

8. How does your church regard/is your church regarded by other churches?

Does your church work together with other churches, or is it so exclusive that it regards all others as inferior? Is its attitude to other churches one of cooperation or confrontation?

9. How easily is your church left?

Can a person leave the church without bringing down upon themselves the criticism and abuse that accompanies those leaving the cults? Is your church content that a person should join another church?

NOTES

Introduction

1. Jan Karel Van Baalen Van Baalen, *Chaos of Cults* (Eerdmans, 1962), p. 14.
2. G. B. Shaw, *Everybody's Political Who's Who*.
3. *Charles Ferguson, The New Books of Revelation*, p.1.
4. *Evening Standard*, 16 February 1995.
5. Ravi Zacharias, *Can Man Live Without God?* (Word, 1994), p. 21.
6. Dr Lee Belford, quoted in Walter Martin, *Kingdom of the Cults* (Bethany House, 1965; 1992), p. 17.
7. Charles Colson, *Who Speaks for God?* (Crossway, 1985)
8. David Wells, *God in the Wasteland*, (IVP, 1994), p. 86.

1. The Definition of Error

1. Ronald Enroth, *A Guide to Cults and New Religions* (IVP, 1993), p. 11.
2. Ronald Enroth, *Churches that Abuse* (Zondervan, 1992), p. 31.
3. Brigham Young, *Journal of Discourses*, vol. 8.
4. Ronald Enroth, op. cit., p. 64.
5. op. cit., p. 177.
6. Steven Hassan, *Combating Cult Mind Control* (Aquarian, 1988), p. 36.
7. Walter Martin, *Kingdom of the Cults* (Bethany House, 1965/1992), p. 29.

8. From Hank Hanegraaff, *Christianity in Crisis* (Harvest House, 1993).

9. Herbert Armstrong, *All About Water Baptism* (Ambassador Press, n.d.), p. 1.

2. The Deceit of Power

1. Jung Chang, *Wild Swans* (Flamingo, 1992), p. 368.

2. Anthony Daniels, *The Wilder Shores of Marx: Journeys in a Vanishing World* (Hutchinson, 1991), p. 70.

3. Ibid. pp. 53–6.

4. Ibid. p. 57.

5. Ronald Enroth, *Churches that Abuse* (Zondervan, 1992), p. 216.

6. Sun Myung Moon, *Divine Principle* p. 16.

7. Joseph Smith, *Pearl of Great Price*, 2; 50.

8. Article entitled 'A Decade of Faith, Hope and Love' in COC's magazine *Discipleship*, Summer, 1989.

9. Benny Hinn, *The Anointing* (Thomas Nelson, 1992), pp. 177–8.

10. Benny Hinn on *Christianity in Crisis* tape by Hank Hanegraaff.

11. Paul Tournier, 'The Power Abusers', *Eternity*, October 1979, p. 25.

12. Ibid.

13. H. Bussell, *Unholy Devotion* (Zondervan, 1983), p. 72.

14. Gary Schaff, 'Suicide Training in the Moon Cult', *New West*, 29 January 1979, p. 63.

15. Jerry Jones, *What Does the Boston Church Teach?* (Mid-America Band and Tape Sales, 1990), vol. 1, pp. 7–8.

16. *The Guardian*, 25 August 1995.

17. Rajneesh, *I Am The Gate* (Harper and Row, 1977), p. 132.

18. Jerry Jones, *What Does The Boston Church Teach?* op. cit., p. 12.

19. John White and Ken Blue, *Healing the Wounded* (IVP, 1985), p. 198.

20. The *Daily Telegraph*, 24 January 1995.

3. The Distortion of Truth

1. Rajneesh, *I Am The Gate* (Harper and Row, 1977), p. 18.
2. *Watchtower*, 15 October 1910.
3. *Time* magazine, 30 September 1974.
4. J. L. Williams, *Contemporary Cults* (New Directions Evangelical Association, n.d.), p. 3.
5. Ronald Enroth, *Churches that Abuse* (Zondervan, 1992), p. 35.
6. *Daily Mail*, 23 August 1995.
7. L. Ron Hubbard, March 1982.
8. The *Daily Telegraph*, 24 April 1995.
9. *Observer*, 14 May 1995.
10. *Making Sure of All Things* (Watchtower Tract and Bible Society), p. 319.

4. The Deception of Innocents

1. EC Report on new religious movements, 1–47 1984.
2. David Wells, *God in the Wasteland* (IVP, 1994), pp. 99–100.
3. *Observer*, 14 May 1995.
4. The *Daily Telegraph* magazine, 11 February 1995.
5. Quoted in Ronald Enroth 'The Power Abusers', *Eternity*, October 1979, p. 25.
6. Article entitled 'A Decade of Faith, Hope and Love', in COC's magazine *Discipleship*, Summer 1989.
7. Ronald Enroth, *Churches that Abuse* (Zondervan, 1992), p. 20.
8. Ibid.
9. The *Daily Telegraph*, 16 March 1995.
10. Albert Speer, *Inside the Third Reich* (Sphere, 1970), p. 49.
11. The *Daily Telegraph* magazine, 11 February 1995.
12. Steven Hassan, *Combating Cult Mind Control* (Aquarian, 1988), p. 42.
13. Charles Colson, *Who Speaks for God?* (Crossway, 1985).

5. The Demand for New Members

1. Chris Elkins, *Heavenly Deception* (Eastbourne, 1982) p. 40.
2. Ronald Enroth, *Churches that Abuse* (Zondervan, 1992), p. 200.
3. Ibid.
4. James Njornstad, *The Moon is not the Son* (Dimension, 1976), p. 104.
5. S. Wookey, *As Angels of Light* (Narrowgate Press, 1990), p. 17.
6. Gloria Copeland, *God's Will is Prosperity* (Harrison House, 1978), p. 54.
7. Hank Hanegraaff, *Christianity in Crisis* (Harvest House, 1993), p. 262.
8. L. Ron Hubbard, 1983.
9. Martin Tierney p. 44.
10. John Ephland, *A Journey Toward Faith*, leaflet issued by Spiritual Counterfeits Project, 1980, p. 5.
11. Dr Bernard Ramm, *Eternity* magazine, November 1963, p. 33.
12. James W. Sire, *Proof-Texting and Scripture-Twisting* (IVP, 1980).
13. Maharishi Mahesh Yogi, *Meditations of Maharishi Mahesh Yogi*, p. 178.
14. Guy Chevreau, *Catch the Fire* (Marshall Pickering, 1994), p. 51.
15. Erik von Daniken, *Chariots of the Gods*, pp. 40–41.
16. C. H. Spurgeon, *Lectures to my Students*,

6. The Destruction of Personality

1. Flavil Yeakley, *The Discipling Dilemma* (Gospel Advocate, 1988), p. 33.
2. Ibid., pp. 34–47.
3. J. R. W. Stott, *I Believe in Preaching* (Hodder & Stoughton, 1982), p. 52.

4. Ronald Enroth, *Churches that Abuse* (Zondervan, 1992), p. 213–14.
5. Ronald Enroth, *A Guide to Cults and New Religions* (IVP, 1993), p. 177.
6. *The Times*, 24 August, 1995.
7. S. Wookey, *As Angels of Light* (Narrowgate Press, 1990), p. 17.
8. *The Times*, op. cit.
9. Steven Hassan, *Combating Cult Mind Control* (Aquarian, 1988), p. 23.
10. Flavil Yeakley, *The Discipling Dilemma* op. cit., pp. 54–5.
11. Ibid.
12. Jerry Jones, *What Does the Boston Church Teach?* (Mid-America Band and Tape Sales, 1990), vol. 1, p. 12.
13. Ibid. vol. 2, p. 84.
14. *Daily Mail*, 26 August 1995.
15. Ronald Enroth, *Churches That Abuse*, op. cit., p. 137.
16. Ibid., p. 40.
17. S. Wookey, *As Angels of Light*, op. cit., p. 17.
18. Martin Tierney, *The New Elect* (Veritas, 1985), p. 46.
19. Ibid., p. 47.
20. Ronald Enroth, *Churches That Abuse*, op. cit., p. 176.
21. Ibid., p. 182.
22. See Ch. 2, n.4.
23. *Observer*, 14 May 1995.

7. The Demise of Error

1. Sun Myung Moon, *Master Speaks*, 17 May 1973.
2. David Berg.
3. *Daily Mail*, 25 August 1995.
4. Ibid.
5. Ronald Enroth, *Churches That Abuse* (Zondervan, 1992), pp. 40–43.
6. Ibid.
7. *Daily Mail*, 26 August 1995.
8. *The Guardian*, 25 August 1995.

9. Tape of Jim Jones at Jonestown, Guyana, 1979.
10. John Allan, *Shopping for a god* (IVP, 1986), p. 133.

8. The Despair of Friends

1. S. Wookey, *As Angels of Light* (Narrowgate Press, 1990), p. 17.
2. Sun Myung Moon, *Christianity in Crisis* (1974), p. 98.
3. Sun Myung Moon, *Divine Principle*, p. 118.
4. S. Wookey, *As Angels of Light* op. cit., p. 17.
5. James Bjornstad, *The Moon is not the Son* (Dimension, 1976), p. 32.
6. Ibid., p. 33.
7. Letter dated 4 April, 1977 sent to the Heritage Chapel in Charleston, Illinois.
8. Fawn Brodie, *No Man Knows My History* (New York, 1957), pp. 29–33.

9. The Danger of Pragmatism

1. Robert Schuller, *Christianity Today*, 5 October, 1984, p. 12.
2. Walter Marin, *Kingdom of the Cults* (Bethany House, 1965/1992), p. 16.
3. The *Daily Telegraph* 26 August 1995.